HOW TO FLY
HELICOPTERS
2ND EDITION

Also by Kas Thomas from TAB BOOKS Inc.

No. 2335 *The Complete Guide to Homebuilt Rotorcraft*

HOW TO FLY
HELICOPTERS
2ND EDITION

LARRY COLLIER, REVISED BY KAS THOMAS

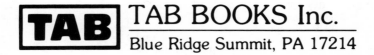

TAB BOOKS Inc.
Blue Ridge Summit, PA 17214

SECOND EDITION

SECOND PRINTING

Copyright © 1986 by TAB BOOKS Inc.

Printed in the United States of America

Reproduction or publication of the content in any manner, without express permission of the publisher, is prohibited. No liability is assumed with respect to the use of the information herein.

First edition copyright © 1979 by TAB BOOKS Inc.

Library of Congress Cataloging in Publication Data

Collier, Larry.
    How to fly helicopters.

    Includes index.
    1. Helicopters—Piloting. I. Thomas, Kas. II. Title.
TL716.5.C64   1986   629.132′5252   85-27840
ISBN 0-8306-0286-0
ISBN 0-8306-2386-8 (pbk.)

Cover photograph courtesy of Schweizer Aircraft.

Contents

Takeoffs and Landings—Hovering, Air Taxiing, and Maneuvering by Ground Reference—Settling with Power—Running Takeoffs, Roll-On Landings, and Quick Stops—Cross-Country Flight—Emergencies

Introduction

What makes a helicopter tick? How do a helicopter's controls work? How does a helicopter "feel" in the air? These questions are being asked with ever greater frequency by would-be helicopter pilots of all ages and backgrounds, but especially by fixed-wing pilots, many of whom have begun to look with new respect at the light helicopter, wondering how hard it is to make the transition to rotary-wing flight.

Helicopters have finally come out of the dark ages, both mechanically and aesthetically, and not surprisingly many airplane pilots find the helicopter's unique capabilities increasingly alluring. Modern light helicopters are as fast as the most popular small planes (i.e., the Cessna 150 and 172) and burn not much more fuel; yet, being VTOL (vertical takeoff or landing) vehicles, they needn't mix with fixed-wing traffic. Helicopters are given expeditious treatment by most control towers and are routinely granted nonstandard arrivals and departures (and direct routings) that fixed-wing pilots could never expect to get. Cross-countries are flown at low altitude (under 1,000 feet) in helicopters, allowing for superb sightseeing. Off-airport landings can be conducted safely, of course, and when the weather goes down, 'copters can often continue to fly safely when most fixed-wing pilots are grounded.

These virtues have not gone unnoticed by a large segment of the fixed-wing community. In fact, many fixed-wing pilots who combine business and pleasure on short (less than 200 miles), low-altitude trips have begun to question whether they need a four-seat airplane at all when a two- or three-seat helicopter might do just as well—or better.

But aren't helicopters supposed to be impossibly difficult to fly? Hovering a helicopter has been likened to patting one's head and rubbing one's stomach while attempting to stand upright on a beach-ball in the deep end of a swimming pool. And certainly many fixed-wing pilots find their first attempts at helicopter flight a humbling experience. Helicopter flying isn't difficult, however, so much as *different*. Like anything else, once you know how to do it, it seems natural.

The process of learning how to fly helicopters is made much easier if you first take the time to study and understand the aero-dynamic forces acting on the helicopter. Unfortunately, there are relatively few easy-to-read-and-understand books on helicopter the-ory of flight (in stark contrast to the situation that exists for fixed-wing flying). Most study guides are either too technical, or too oriented to the FAA written test, or don't say enough about how a helicopter "feels" in flight in the cockpit to help the novice form a gut-level impression of how a helicopter really does what it does. And yet, without a firm intuitive understanding of helicopter flight principles, it is impossible for the beginner to make rapid progress as a student. This is because helicopters, lacking the aerodynamic control feedback and built-in stability of fixed-wing aircraft, are not "seat of the pants" flying machines; learning to fly helicopters is not something that comes with simple repetition of tasks involv-ing minor hand-eye coordination. Helicopter flying is a largely in-tellectual process, drawing not only on the pilot's kinesthetic senses but also his or her ability to trend-extrapolate in four dimensions, in real time. This is not something that can be learned overnight. The new helicopter pilot needs all the help he or she can get.

This book is an attempt to bridge the gap between theory and practice for the beginning helicopter pilot so as to make the transi-tion to rotary-wing flight more "natural" (and less mysterious). It is also an attempt to fill a void in the publishing field. Few other books (certainly none in this one's price range) bring together the combination of historical background, aerodynamic theory, and practical hands-on advice that the present book does. The 206-page first edition of this book proved quite popular for its no-nonsense, simplified "here's how" approach to helicopter flight, combining thoroughness and readability with ample illustration of key points.

The present edition represents a significant expansion of the highly successful first edition. The history and aerodynamics chapters have been completely rewritten, other chapters expanded, and two new chapters added on maintenance and taking the FAA flight test. In addition, many new photos have been used, and the entire text updated to reflect the increasingly widespread use of the Robinson R-22 in flight training (a helicopter that had barely come into existence when the first edition was being written). So the present edition can essentially be considered a new book, for all practical purposes.

In writing this book we have made every attempt to concentrate on theory where it is needed, but an attempt is also made to convey the ineluctable wonderment and sheer gut satisfaction of helicopter flying. If *How to Fly Helicopters* aids your progress as a student, it will have served its main purpose. If it adds to your enjoyment of flying, it will have been a double success.

1

In the Beginning

The history of helicopter flight is a long and delightfully complex one—longer and more complex, certainly, than the history of fixed-wing (airplane) flight. The word *helicopter*, in fact (combining the Greek words *heliko*, meaning spiral-like, and *pteron*, for wing), had come into the English language long before the Wright brothers flew. The Wright brothers themselves built and flew tiny helicopter models as far back as 1878, later abandoning the idea of mechanized vertical flight as too difficult. (Bishop Milton Wright, father of Orville and Wilbur, had once brought home a copterlike toy top for the boys to play with; Wilbur would tell a friend many years later that he and his brother "made many more of these small toys, fashioning the blades of bamboo and tissue paper, and we flew them with great success.")

An Ancient Dream

The first inventor to seriously propose a detailed design for a helical-wing device capable of lifting a human occupant vertically was Leonardo da Vinci, whose well-known "aerial screw" sketches first appeared around 1490 (Fig. 1-1). Da Vinci himself seemed remarkably confident of the screw's ability to fly, describing it as follows: "I say that this instrument, made with a helix and well made, that is to say of flaxen linen of which one has closed the pores with starch, and turned with a great speed, said helix is able to make

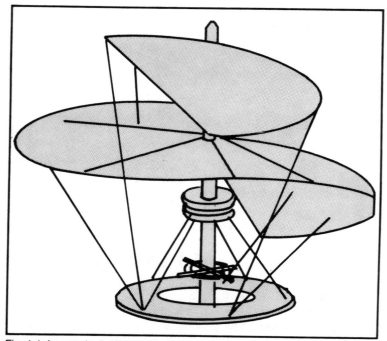

Fig. 1-1. Leonardo da Vinci's famous aerial screw represented one of the first serious proposals for a VTOL vehicle.

a screw in the air and to climb high.'' Some historians go so far as to say that da Vinci built and flew small models of the aerial screw using paper and wire, although there is no verifiable record of this.

The first model helicopter conceded to have flown under its own power (excluding the so-called Chinese tops mentioned in Oriental literature) was the one demonstrated by the Frenchmen Launoy and Beinvenu at the World's Fair in Paris in 1784 (Fig. 1-2). This ambitious toy, employing counterrotating turkey feathers, is said to have routinely reached altitudes of 70 feet or more, and stirred considerable interest among inventors and scientists of the day. One of those influenced by the toy's success was the Englishman Sir George Cayley, who built replicas of the Launoy-Bienvenu device (and saw them reach heights of 90 feet or more) before proposing an elaborate helicopter model of his own design in 1843. The famous Cayley model, featuring lateral twin booms (and a beaklike nose), used a small steam engine to develop power for the four eight-bladed rotors (Fig. 1-3), but the engine proved too weak and the Cayley copter never flew. Cayley's design did stir the imaginations of his contemporaries, however, and so provided impetus for further important VTOL (vertical takeoff or landing) research.

The Dream Takes Shape

One of those who had followed Cayley's progress with keen interest was an Italian civil engineering professor by the name of Enrico Forlanini. In 1878, Forlanini succeeded in constructing (and flying) a dual-contrarotating-rotors machine powered by a quarter-horsepower steam engine (Fig. 1-4). The model weighed approximately eight pounds and is said to have achieved a height of 40 feet in flight trials, remaining there for extended periods before running out of fuel.

Fig. 1-2. Launoy and Bienvenu demonstrated a rubber-powered toy helicopter similar to this one at the World's Fair in Paris in 1784.

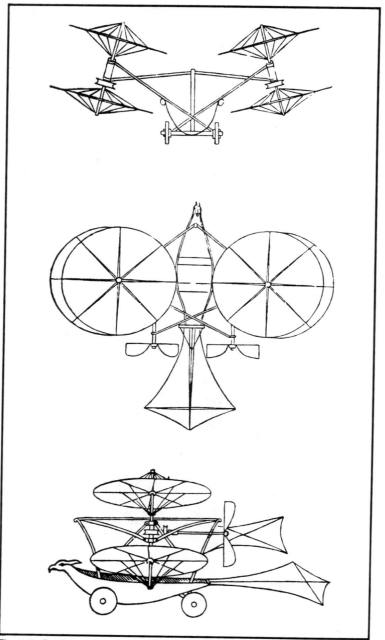

Fig. 1-3. Sir George Cayley's three-view of his helicopter model, which was demonstrated in 1843 but never actually flew.

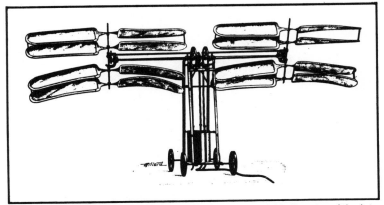

Fig. 1-4. Enrico Forlanini's 1/4-hp, contrarotating coaxial helicopter of the late 1800s.

Other unsuccessful designs, the Castel helicopter and the Owen machine, are shown in Figs. 1-5 and 1-6.

The first man-carrying helicopter to achieve flight appears to have been the very large (yet aerodynamically efficient) machine constructed by the Frenchman Louis Breguet in 1907. This unique copter employed four large (20-foot diameter) non-overlapping rotors, each with four pairs of blades mounted two deep, in biplane fashion. Although highly unstable, the Breguet device did lift a man off the ground (briefly)—to an altitude of about two feet. Unfortunately, to accomplish this with any safety, it was necessary to have four men stationed near the machine with poles ready to right the craft should it begin to tip. Unable to improve the controllability of his ship, Breguet would in subsequent years go on to achieve distinction in the field of aeroplane design before returning to helicopters again late in life.

Helicopter Pioneers

Barely two months after Breguet's widely publicized "helicoplane flight," fellow countryman Paul Cornu took to the air with a twin-rotor, 24-horsepower machine weighing a mere 573 pounds. Unlike Breguet's craft, Cornu's helicopter, although unstable, was not steadied in flight by ground observers; hence, some historians believe Cornu's device to be the first man-carrying helicopter worthy of the name. The Cornu copter carried its human occupant ("pilot" is perhaps overstating it) to heights of a few feet at a speed of 6 mph.

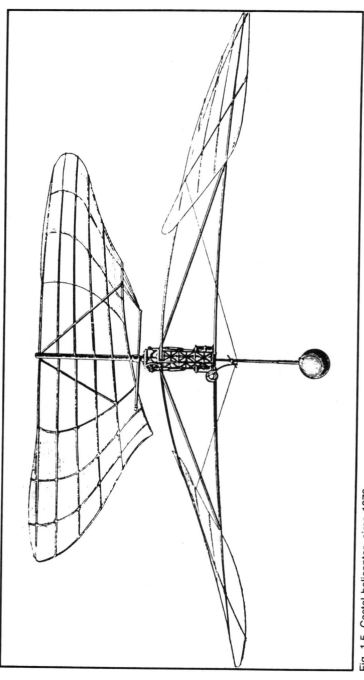

Fig. 1-5. Castel helicopter, circa 1878.

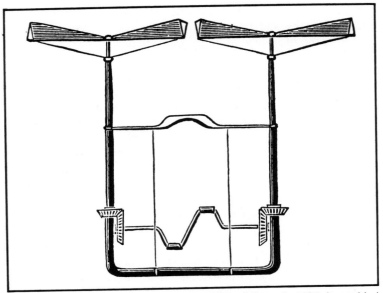

Fig. 1-6. This machine was proposed by Richard Owen in 1885. It provided for the pilot and lifting screws operated by foot power.

Igor Sikorsky, later to become a giant in the industry, built two model helicopters in czarist Russia in 1909 and 1910, the first of which didn't fly at all, and the second of which lifted nothing more than its own weight. Disheartened, Sikorsky subsequently turned his talents to fixed-wing design, an area which brought him considerable success, particularly with heavy bombers and (later) seaplanes. Among his other distinctions, Sikorsky built and flew the first multi-engine airplane in 1913. When he arrived in the U. S. in 1919, Sikorsky worked briefly for the Army's experimental aircraft station at McCook Field but was advised, after being let go, to attempt to find work in another area, as aviation was "a dying industry." He would go on, of course, to virtually invent the U. S. helicopter industry singlehandedly in 1938.

In 1916, a Lt. Petroczy and Professor von Karmon of Austria constructed a contrarotating coaxial helicopter with three 40-hp engines driving 20-foot rotors. The craft was used as an observation platform; three cables were attached to it in such a way that they would unreel from a ground control unit as the machine climbed vertically. Mounted above the rotating blades, a crow's-nest-type structure served as the observer's compartment. Before the cables were sufficiently taut on takeoff, the machine proved to be dangerously unstable. But with slack taken up, the craft was quite airworthy and reportedly made numerous reconnaissance flights, some of nearly an hour in duration.

In the U. S., Emile Berliner, a prolific inventor whose credits include the gramophone and microphone, teamed up with his son Henry (who had learned to fly in the Army) to build a coaxial helicopter with small-diameter fixed-pitch rotors in 1919. This machine, with vanes in the rotor slipstream for directional control, proved very unstable but did fly successfully for periods of up to several minutes. Three years later, after his father retired due to ill health, Henry Berliner experimented with a design of his own, removing the wings from a French Nieuport fighter and replacing them with struts to hold solid, propeller-like rotors that would turn in opposite directions. This aircraft (a forerunner in configuration to the world's first truly controllable helicopter, the Focke-Achgelis FW-61 of 1936) flew reasonably well in a demonstration flight in Washington, D.C. on June 16, 1922, but its stability problems eventually persuaded its creator to abandon helicopters for fixed-wing designs.

The Roaring Twenties inaugurated a period of vigorous experimentation in rotary-winged flight, both at home and abroad. NACA (the National Advisory Committee for Aeronautics), had been established by Congress in 1915 for "the scientific study of the problems of flight," the Frenchman Etienne Edmond Oemichen had won 90,000 francs in an open competition for the design of a successful helicopter, and in the U. S. the Army announced its first contract for a VTOL aircraft.

The latter is worthy of some comment. Russian-born scientist George de Bothezat, having convinced Army officials that he had developed a successful helicopter in Russia and could bring it to full fruition in the U. S., signed a contract with the Army which saw de Bothezat get $5,000 for the first complete set of drawings for a helicopter, $4,800 more for the detailed design and construction, and a $2,500 bonus if the machine actually flew! (If, by some stroke of brilliant design, the machine were to rise 300 feet and descend safely with the engine throttled, the inventor was to get an extra $7,500.) These were of course fantastic sums of money for the day, but the Wrights had gotten $25,000 for delivery of the first airplane to the Army in 1908, so the amounts were not totally out of line. Besides which, de Bothezat had proclaimed: "I am the world's greatest scientist and outstanding mathematician."

The de Bothezat helicopter, built in utmost secrecy at McCook

Field in Dayton, Ohio, was a mechanical monstrosity and—at 3,585 pounds—easily the heaviest helicopter of its day. Powered by a 180-hp (later 220-hp) Le Rhone engine, the "flying octopus" (as it was dubbed by bemused onlookers) featured four non-overlapping six-bladed rotors, each 22 feet in diameter. It was a maze of steel and aluminum trusswork, replete with guy wires, gears, and push-pull tubes. "There was so much framework structure," one engineer was heard to remark, "that you had to see the drawings before you could find the operator, and he looked as though he were behind bars."

On December 18, 1922, the de Bothezat helicopter hovered at an altitude of six feet for one minute and 42 seconds, a not insignificant achievement for the time. The machine would go on to make more than 100 flights in all over a period of several years (with de Bothezat supervising many improvements to the design). After spending over $200,000 on the craft, however, the Army abandoned the de Bothezat helicopter as too unwieldy and complex in addition to being uncontrollable in the event of a power-train failure. The prototype craft was ultimately dismantled for scrap, and de Bothezat retired a dejected man.

Autogyros

In Spain, meanwhile, very significant research in rotorcraft stability and control was underway at the hands of the Marquis de Pescara and another Spanish aristocrat, Juan de la Cierva. Pescara built several large coaxial-rotor helicopters which achieved control by cyclic variation of the pitch of the blades. In 1923 a Pescara machine established a helicopter record by flying a quarter of a mile under full control. An agile craft by existing standards, the Pescara (powered by a 180-hp Hispano-Suiza engine) could be test-flown inside a large hangar, and often was.

By far the most important design breakthroughs of the era, however, were those being pioneered by Juan de la Cierva in Madrid in the period 1919 to 1923. During this period, Cierva struggled with a new concept in aircraft: an aeroplane with a conventional forward-thrusting propeller and engine, very tiny wings (just big enough to provide lateral control), and a large overhead rotor that would provide lift simply by freewheeling. Since it was not designed to take off straight up or hover, the craft could not be considered a helicopter; in fact, Cierva coined the term "autogiro" (similar machines, built by others, were "autogyros") to describe the device. Cierva had discovered that the freewheeling rotor allowed for very slow, soft, almost vertical landings, while also providing benign control and stability characteristics (quite in contrast to powered rotor systems). In flight, the autogiro flew very much like an airplane, with a stick and rudder that responded to control inputs as an airplane would. In the event of an engine failure, however, the autogiro would simply float down to earth softly, with the rotor continuing to windmill (or autorotate) of its own accord—in contrast to an airplane, which of course could (if the pilot panicked and made a wrong control input) stall and/or spin in.

Cierva's first autogiros were not successful; he found that on reaching a high enough runway speed for takeoff, the entire machine would rock hard over to one side, out of control. Cierva built a number of rubber-band models until he hit upon the solution. What he discovered was that the extra lift experienced by the rotor's advancing, or forward-moving, blades (combined with the deficit or lift given by the same blades during the *downwind* portion of their travel) resulted in unequal lift distribution across the rotor disc. In other words, one side of the rotor disc was creating more lift than the other side whenever the aircraft was moving into the wind at any speed more than a few mph. Since the blades were rigidly attached to the spindle shaft, the resulting aerodynamic forces acted to bank the entire aircraft over to one side.

Cierva eventually came upon the answer to the "asymmetric lift" problem when he invented what's now known as the *flapping hinge*. In short, Cierva discovered that he could eliminate the effects of asymmetric lift by providing a hinge at the spindle attachment of each blade such that the blade would be free to flap (or "cone") upward or downward, much as a bird's wing can flap up or down. In flight, centrifugal forces would keep the blades more or less perpendicular to the rotor shaft, but during each trip of the rotor blade around the machine, it would automatically adjust its vertical position, seeking just the right "coning angle" to allow lift equalization across the disc. In forward flight, the advancing blade would rise as it developed more lift; then it would fall an equal amount 180 degrees later while moving through the "retreating" portion of the disc. In this way, lift forces would balance out, and the craft would stay upright.

The principle of the flapping hinge would be of far-reaching importance to helicopter designers in subsequent years, but the initial impact of the development was to make the autogyro far and away the most successful type of rotorcraft in the world from 1923 to 1936. During this period, Cierva crossed the English Channel in an autogiro (doing so at an average speed of 100 mph—phenomenal for a rotary-wing aircraft); Amelia Earhart set a rotorcraft altitude record of 18,400 feet in an autogiro, and an autogiro became the first rotary-wing aircraft to land aboard a ship. In the U. S., Harold F. Pitcairn won the Collier Trophy for his work with autogyros (Fig. 1-7). Cierva modified an autogiro to have a so-called "jump takeoff" (vertical liftoff) capability, giving very nearly helicopter performance. These developments caused the inventor Thomas Edison to hail the autogyro as "the greatest advance that could have been made in aviation."

As successful as the autogyro was, there was still one thing it could not do: namely, hover motionless in the air. As a result, research into vertical flight continued, and with the appearance of the first truly practical helicopters in the late 1930s, the autogyro quickly fell into obscurity. (Another setback to the autogyro's cause was Cierva's untimely death in the weather-related 1936 crash of an airliner near London.)

The First Practical Helicopters

Among the pioneers to finally bring the helicopter out of the dark ages was Louis Breguet, who returned to helicopter experimentation in 1931, this time with notable success. One Breguet

Fig. 1-7. Pitcairn autogyro. The autogyro's main rotor is freewheeling (not powered), turning more or less by pinwheel action—so the machine is, in effect, always in "autorotation."

machine in particular (oddly named in Gyroplane Laboratoire) made headlines, reaching speeds of 67 mph in cruise and climbing to an altitude of 500 feet under good control. On one flight, the 350-hp, coaxial-rotor helicopter remained aloft for 45 minutes. Breguet set world records for altitude, speed, endurance, and distance in the last years before World War II, but as luck would have it many of his achievements were overshadowed by world events—and by brash counterclaims of superior helicopter achievements by the Nazis.

In Germany, a twin-rotor helicopter called the Focke-Achgelis FW-61 made numerous noteworthy flights between 1937 and 1939, ultimately breaking all existing international records and gaining widespread recognition as the first truly successful helicopter in the world. The Nazis, well aware of the positive public relations value of the craft, kindled the imaginations of newsreel watchers everywhere by releasing movie footage of the FW-61 being flown *indoors* (inside the Deutschland Halle in Berlin) at the hands of a female test pilot, Hanna Reitsch. Maneuvering the helicopter backwards, forwards, and sideways (and performing 360-degree hovering turns with ease), Reitsch amply demonstrated the FW-61's superb agility, proving once and for all that controllability problems need never again hinder the progress of helicopter design— at least, not in Nazi Germany.

Some of the FW-61's records included:

☐ Duration—1:20:49
☐ Distance—143.069 miles in a straight line
☐ Altitude—11,243 feet
☐ Speed—76 mph

Another important first for the FW-61: The Focke-Achgelis was the first helicopter to demonstrate safe power-off autorotations. (Louis Breguet would also demonstrate this capability in 1937.)

In 1941, Anton Flettner further bolstered Nazi pride with the introduction of a fast, highly maneuverable intermeshing-rotor helicopter, the Flettner 282. Like the FW-61, the Flettner 282 used a 160-hp Siemens-Halske Sh.14A radial engine to drive two counterrotating rotors. However, instead of mounting the rotors in non-overlapping fashion on the ends of long lateral booms (as in the FW-61), Flettner achieved impressive weight and space savings by intermeshing the ship's two-bladed, 39-foot-diameter rotors in eggbeater fashion, angling each mast outboard by about ten degrees. Although contracts were let for the production of 1,000 of these helicopters in 1944, only about 30 were actually built by the war's end. (The FW-61, by contrast, was never put into production.)

The U. S. military, anxious to have its own version of the Focke-Achgelis helicopter (or something just as good), contracted with the Platt-LePage Aircraft Company in 1940 to produce a twin-rotor, lateral-boom, T-tailed-fuselage helicopter very similar in layout to the famous FW-61. Three years and $200,000 later, the Platt-LePage XR-1A achieved most of its design goals and was deemed a success, but the Army had by that time investigated other helicopter configurations and was committed in other areas, so the Platt-LePage design never saw production.

Having achieved tremendous success in the design of fixed-wing aircraft (the Pan Am Clippers, for example), Igor Sikorsky returned to rotorcraft experimentation in 1938, focusing his efforts on perfecting a single-rotor configuration. The prototype's design called for the placement of small additional control rotors on the tail boom to counteract the torque generated by the main rotor—a now-familiar arrangement (Fig. 1-8). Sikorsky's prototype, the VS300, not only flew successfully (its first flight was at the hands of Sikorsky himself on September 14, 1939), but on May 6, 1941, broke the world endurance record held by the Focke-Achgelis

Fig. 1-8. Donning his ubiquitous fedora, Igor Sikorsky attempts a tethered test flight of an early single-rotor helicopter (probably in 1938).

helicopter, remaining aloft for 1:32:36—almost 12 minutes better than the FW-61.

Sikorsky spent approximately three years working out various control problems with the VS300, but even before final modifications were worked out (if indeed it can be said of any helicopter that "final modifications" are ever made), Sikorsky's fledgling company was hard at work on a production helicopter for the military, the R-4. During World War II, the R-4 saw service with the U. S. Army, Navy, and Coast Guard in addition to British forces, mostly as a patrol aircraft, but also in a rescue role.

The Helicopter Comes of Age

With the end of World War II began what could only be called an explosion of helicopter research and development activities, with aircraft companies of all sizes (from one-man on up) testing virtually every conceivable bizarre configuration of rotary-wing aircraft. Altogether something like 300 companies were engaged in helicopter R&D during the postwar period. Most, of course, foundered.

The most successful postwar helicopter, the Bell 47, actually had its roots in a 1943 design that saw manufacture by Bell Aircraft under the direction of Arthur Young. The very first Bell helicopter, the experimental Model 30, struggled into the air in mid-1943 and was followed by an improved version (which became the 47) in December 1945. The trademark characteristic of the Bell 47 (which was otherwise similar in configuration to the Sikorsky VS300) was and is the familiar Bell two-bladed main rotor system with its small stabilizer bar oriented at right angles to the main rotor blades. The stabilizer-bar rotor and fishbowl-like one-piece plexiglass, cockpit enclosure would become familiar sights in the 1950s as Bell turned out more than 5,000 Model 47 variants. A two- to three-place side-by-side aircraft, the Model 47 initially came with a 178-hp Franklin engine but in later versions would use a variety of other powerplants. The Bell 47's CAA (Civil Aeronautics Authority) Type Certificate, granted March 8, 1946, was the first ever awarded to a commercial helicopter anywhere in the world. The fact that many hundreds of these machines are still in daily operation is a testament to the soundness of Arthur Young's original design (Fig. 1-9).

In 1944, at age 19, Stanley Hiller Jr. designed and built the first American helicopter to successfully use a counterrotating rotor system, the XH-44. Although it flew well, the two-place XH-44 was involved in a nearly catastrophic non-injury crash in 1946, and sub-

Fig. 1-9. The first civil helicopter to gain CAA (now FAA) production approval was the Bell 47. The Bell 47 was the most successful postwar helicopter of them all, with more than 5,000 ships eventually produced.

sequently Hiller turned his energies toward the development of a lighter, single-rotor-type helicopter design. The result was a two-bladed helicopter known as the Model 360, similar in size and layout to the Bell 47 but having an overhead control stick and featuring an aerodynamic servo-control bar (the "Rotor-Matic" control system) where the Bell's stabilizer bar would normally be. In the production version, the 178-hp three-place machine was dubbed the UH-12 and received CAA (now FAA) Type Approval on October 14, 1948. Thanks partly to the outbreak of the Korean War, more than 2,000 Hiller 12-series helicopters were eventually produced. Many are still in operation today.

Hiller over the years produced several interesting designs on a one-off basis for the military, including a flying platform (a saucer-like hovercraft with the pilot standing above the rotor disc), a collapsible overhead-control mini-copter called the Rotorcycle, and the Hiller Hornet (not to be confused with McDonnell's Little Henry), a tiny one-man machine featuring ramjet engines at the tips of the two rotor blades. All flew successfully.

In 1943, after the Platt-LePage helicopter failed to reach production, one of the young engineers who had worked on the XR-1 project, Frank Piasecki, designed and built his own helicopter, a small single-rotor ship (with conventional tail rotor) powered by a 90-hp Franklin. By February 1944, Piasecki had secured a U. S. Navy contract to produce what would turn out to be the first practical fore-and-aft tandem-rotor helicopter, the XHRP-1. Thus began a long series of adventures into tandem-rotor designs. The advantages of the tandem-rotor layout (other than that of efficient torque counteraction by the opposite-turning rotors) include low drag profile, low structural weight compared to lateral-rotor designs of the Focke-Achgelis type, and extremely wide center-of-gravity envelope (or CG range). Most helicopters, including the lateral-boom type, are exceedingly sensitive to noseheavy or tail-heavy conditions—so much so that loading is very critical. With a tandem-rotor aircraft, however, noseheaviness or tailheaviness is readily correctable, inasmuch as the rotor at the "heavy" end of the ship can easily be made to work harder. Hence, many of the world's heavy-lift helicopters are of the tandem-rotor, "flying banana" configuration.

The Piasecki helicopters were behemoths of the industry, and superb designs even by present standards. The original Flying Banana, the Piasecki HRP-1, first flew in prototype form in March 1945. The U. S. Navy bought 20 HRP-1 aircraft for use aboard ships in the late 1940s. This model, powered by a 600-hp Pratt & Whitney R-1340 radial engine, had 41-foot-diameter, three-bladed rotors at the ends of a 48-foot-long fuselage. Gross weight was an impressive 8,000 pounds. A slightly more compact offshoot of the HRP-1, the HUP-2 (powered by a 550-hp Continental radial mill), saw widespread use with the Army as well as the Navy in the years just after the Korean War, with 339 helicopters delivered. The HUP-2 design differed most significantly from the HRP-1 in that the fore and aft rotors overlapped each other on the HUP-2 (the rear one was higher than the front rotor), while on the HRP-1 the rotors were non-overlapping.

An upscaled version of Piasecki's HRP-1, the H-21 Work Horse, was built in the hundreds during the 1950s and saw use in Vietnam before retiring from military service in 1963. The H-21's non-overlapping 44-foot rotors and 1,425-hp Wright R-1820 engine made it an impressive machine, with a maximum takeoff weight of 13,500 pounds. As early as 1953 one of these helicopters established international records for speed (146.7 mph) and altitude (22,289 feet).

As if these successes weren't enough, Piasecki startled the helicopter world in 1952 with the unveiling of the YH-16A, which had the double distinction of not only being the largest helicopter in the world (with twin 119-foot-wide, three-bladed rotors), but also among the first jet-turbine powered helicopters in the air. (Another jet-powered helicopter that came on the scene at about the same time was the Kaman 225. It is not clear which one flew under jet power first.) Primarily a research vehicle not intended for production, the YH-16A showed that it was practical to build helicopters capable of carrying 50 people or more. Unfortunately, the sole YH-16A prototype was destroyed in a crash involving failure of the main drive shaft interconnecting the twin rotors and was never rebuilt.

In 1956, Piasecki changed his helicopter company's name to Vertol, and work on a new overlapping-rotor design was begun, culminating in the introduction of the extremely successful CH-47 Chinook (now produced by Boeing). More than 500 twin-turbine Chinooks have been produced, many under foreign license.

Piasecki was not the only one to exploit the fore-and-aft rotor layout; the first CAA (FAA) production approval to be granted to a tandem-rotor helicopter actually went to the McCulloch MC-4, whose development can be traced to the JOV-3 prototype of 1946. The MC-4, a four-place ship powered by a 200-hp Franklin engine, had twin three-bladed rotors of 23-foot diameter and flew at a gross weight of 2,300 pounds (at speeds to 105 mph). The U. S. Army bought three MC-4 aircraft for evaluation, but no subsequent military contracts were let, and the civilian market proved disappointing, so despite the resurrection of the machine under the "Jovair Sedan 4E" name in the early 1960s, very few of these helicopters were ever built.

The MC-4 is important for another reason, however. The creator of this machine, D. K. Jovanovich, would play a pivotal role in the design of two other FAA Type Certificated rotorcraft: the Hughes 269 (certificated April 9, 1959) and the McCulloch J-2 gyroplane (the last autogyro to see production in this country, circa 1972). The rotor systems of the MC-4, Hughes 269A, and J-2 are all nearly identical.

Two American manufacturers were able to successfully exploit the eggbeater-type intermeshing-rotor configuration pioneered by Anton Flettner (discussed earlier in the context of the Flettner 282) after World War II. One manufacturer, Kellett, had built autogyros in the 1930s and 40s; around 1950 it introduced a large eggbeater-type copter with 65-foot-diameter three-bladed rotors under the designation XH-10. This helicopter, with not one but two 525-hp

Continental engines, was capable of hefting 15,000 pounds and could fly on one engine to 4,600 feet. No large military orders were placed, however, and the machine quickly fell into obscurity along with its parent company.

A second firm to exploit the intermeshing-rotors approach (this time with considerable success) was Kaman. The piston-powered HTK-1, Kaman's first intermeshing design, flew in the late 1940s and quickly established itself as a successful design. Unlike the Kellett XH-10 (above), the Kaman helicopter used a two-bladed teetering rotor, and in direct contrast to others who used the two-bladed teetering rotor approach (Bell, Hiller, etc.), control of rotor blade pitch changes was effected not through the standard tilting swashplate arrangement (to be discussed in greater detail in Chapter 4), but instead by means of tiny controllable trim tabs on the tailing edges of the blades—a mechanically simple, aerodynamically effective innovation.

The main advantage of the intermeshing-rotor configuration is that since each rotor is turning opposite the other, torque effects are counteracted without the need of a long tail boom and tail rotor. At the same time, since there are no long lateral booms or fuselage structures needed to separate the rotors, weight is saved and the helicopter is overall very compact. This in turn makes possible greater payloads and higher top speeds. In addition, the symmetric lift (and torque) of the rotors makes the Kaman-type helicopter very easy to fly.

Unfortunately, this latter characteristic effectively banned the Kaman copters from a trainer role. Because its other line helicopters were of the Sikorsky-type conventional-tail-rotor configuration (which is much harder to fly), the U. S. Air Force ruled out any role for the Kaman ships as trainers—they were "too easy" to fly, and pilots checked out in the Kamans could not transition quickly to other types. Nevertheless, Kaman's queer-looking wide-bodied eggbeater-copters saw widespread use among three branches of the military service in this country, and several others around the world, in firefighting and rescue roles. The turbine-powered H-43 in particular (first flown in 1958) proved very popular, with 264 military models built for seven countries (Fig. 1-10).

For a trainer, the U. S. military would turn to a small, two-place machine originally developed as a private venture in 1955 by the Aircraft Division of the Hughes Tool Company. The Hughes 269 first flew in October 1956, gained FAA approval in April 1959, and went into production as the 269A in July 1960. Within the next

Fig. 1-10. The turbine-powered Kaman H-43 saw service with three branches of the U. S. military, mostly in a search-and-rescue capacity. The two-bladed, semi-rigid, teetering rotors of the H-43 were canted about 15 degrees apart and turned in opposite directions, intermeshing eggbeater-style. Despite the craft's odd appearance, it performed well and was easy to fly—so easy to fly, in fact, that the military rejected it as a training ship.

eight years, the U. S. Army ordered 791 of the copters for primary-training duties at its Fort Rucker, Alabama, base. Hundreds more entered the civilian market, where the machine became the most important civil trainer (along with the Bell 47) of the 1960s and 70s.

The Hughes 269A and 269B (or 300) are respectively two- and three-place single-rotor machines powered by a non-supercharged Lycoming HIO-360 engine developing either 180 or 190 horse-power. Power is transmitted to the three-bladed rotor by means of eight rubber vee-belts. The 300 differs from the 269A in having slightly longer main rotor blades (27-foot-diameter vs. the 269A's 25-foot-diameter), higher gross weight, bigger tail rotor, and a higher-horsepower engine, among other details. The 300C is still in production; its manufacturer is now Schweizer Aircraft of Elmira, New York (Fig. 1-11).

A contemporary of the Hughes 269A that sold well initially before falling on hard times in the late 1960s is the Brantly B-2B. A somewhat smaller ship than the 269A, the Brantly B-2B gets its

Fig. 1-11. The Hughes 269 got its start in the late 1950s as a purely commercial venture, but within a few years of its introduction the U. S. Army had ordered almost 800 of these tiny copters for use as trainers.

power from a vertically mounted 180-hp Lycoming engine (the 269A/300 engine is horizontally mounted, by contrast), driving a three-bladed rotor of somewhat unconventional design in that there are two flapping hinges per blade—one at the roof (per usual) and another at mid-blade (actually, 52 inches out from the hub). The original B-2 prototype first flew on February 21, 1953, but was not FAA certificated until six years later. Within the first four years of production, over 200 completed aircraft were delivered (Figs. 1-12, 1-13). By 1966, however, the company's founders had sold out to the Lear Jet Corporation (now Gates Learjet), after which sales virtually stopped. Entrepreneur Michael Hynes eventually acquired the rights to the Brantly series and has continued to produce parts for the ship from the new company headquarters in Frederick, Oklahoma, even manufacturing a few new aircraft for sale. Sales of the B-2B continue to be depressed, however, although a good many can always be found on the used market.

In addition to the B-2 series, Brantly got FAA approval to build an enlarged, five-passenger variant known as the Model 305, with tricycle-wheel landing gear. Only a few dozen of the larger utility model were ever built, although in recent years the U. S. military has ordered several for ECM (electronic countermeasures) drone research.

Fig. 1-12. The original Brantly B-1 prototype (circa 1946) was a coaxial helicopter. It never entered production.

Still another three-bladed piston helicopter to meet with fair success in the civil marketplace is the Enstrom F-28/F-280 series. Like the Hughes 300, the Enstrom F-28 uses a horizontally mounted, 360-cubic-inch, four-cylinder fuel-injected Lycoming engine to drive a single three-blade main rotor (and two-blade tail rotor) via pulley action, but in the Enstrom's case only one large

Fig. 1-13. The Brantly B-2 prototype (1952) sported conventional landing gear and an ice cream cone-like fuselage. Two flapping hinges were used per blade.

rubber belt is used, rather than eight smaller belts as in the 300 or 269A. In contrast to the 269A/300, the Enstrom utilizes a fully enclosed engine compartment and tail boom, and on the whole is a much larger machine than either the 269A or Brantly B-2B. There are other substantial differences as well. The Enstrom, for example, has extremely stout main rotor blades (weighing 51 pounds each) with unlimited service life. (The Hughes and Brantly copters have limited-life blades.) Also, the Enstrom is available in turbocharged as well as unturbocharged versions (which the others are not), and the basic engine is rated for additional horsepower: 205-hp to 225-hp, depending on the exact model. Various aerodynamic, styling, and mechanical differences serve to differentiate the F-28 series from the F-280 Shark series. Next to the Hughes/Schweizer 300C and Robinson R-22 (see below), the Enstrom F-28 remains one of the most popular training and general-purpose helicopters in the U. S. today.

The last "clean sheet of paper" piston helicopter design to receive FAA Type Certification (and achieve success in the civil marketplace) is the Robinson R-22. A two-passenger machine designed with simplicity and long service life foremost in mind, the Robinson uses a Lycoming 0-320 engine (of either 150 or 160 horsepower, depending on whether the helicopter is a straight R-22 or the later R-22HP), mounted horizontally and partially enclosed, to drive a two-bladed, non-stabilized rotor system. At approximately $85,000

Fig. 1-14. With a maximum takeoff weight of 70,000 pounds, the Sikorsky YCH-53E is currently the biggest operational helicopter in the free world. The machine employs three turboshaft engines to drive a 7-bladed, titanium rotor.

new, the Robinson R-22 is the least expensive helicopter being manufactured in the world today, and it is fast becoming the most popular civil trainer. We will have more to say about the Robinson R-22 throughout this book.

Aside from the Schweizer 300C, the Enstroms, and the Robinson R-22, all other production helicopters in the U. S. are turbine (jet) powered, rather than piston-powered (Fig. 1-14). The most popular light turbine helicopters include the Bell 206 JetRanger (Fig. 1-15) and LongRanger, the Hughes/McDonnell-Douglas 500D, and the Fairchild-Hiller 1100—all three outgrowths of designs submitted for the U. S. Army Light Observation Helicopter competition of the early Vietnam era. The advantages of turbine power for light helicopters are primarily due to the turbine's light weight and reliability. (The service life of a turbine engine is typically two to three times that of a piston engine.) On the downside, however, are cost and fuel consumption. While many older turbine helicopters are available on the used market for under $200,000, most turbine ships are too expensive for the typical private owner to operate, and for this reason we will limit our discussions in this book primarily to piston helicopter operation (especially since that is where most training is done anyway). There is little question, however, that

Fig. 1-15. The Bell JetRanger, a tremendous success in the civil market, was originally an outgrowth of the Army's LOH (Light Observation Helicopter) competition of the early 1960s.

in the future, the benefits of turbine operation will spread to encompass virtually all helicopter flying, since the increasing price curve of the piston engine is bound to cross over the decreasing price curve of turbine powerplants.

With the recent advances in carbon-fiber, foam, plastic, and Kevlar structures, civil helicopters have made important gains in component life, dispatch reliability, payload, and cost of operation, to say nothing of performance. Speeds and comfort levels that were once thought to be impossible for helicopters are now commonplace; within the space of little more than 60 years, design goals that daunted the best of inventors (including da Vinci and the Wright brothers) have been surpassed. Where the next half-century will lead is anyone's guess.

2

Basic Aerodynamics

Any heavier-than-air vehicle that flies—whether rotary-wing, fixed-wing, motorized, or glider—does so through the use of airfoils. With them, an aircraft is able to generate enough lift to get off the ground; once airborne, airfoils are used to maneuver the aircraft, climb, descend, and land. Without airfoils, flying would be difficult or even impossible. Let us take a look at what an airfoil is and why it is so basic to flight.

Airfoil

An *airfoil* is any device that has been shaped in such a way as to produce lift when air is moved across it. (In the abstract, an airfoil is the shape itself, rather than the object.) Almost anything is capable of producing a certain amount of lift when exposed to a large airflow. Even the proverbial barn door will fly, given a big enough gust of wind. NASA (National Aeronautics and Space Administration) research in the 1960s and 1970s with so-called "lifting body" devices proved that wingless aircraft—if shaped correctly, and flown at high enough speeds—can generate enough lift to allow controlled flight.

In the context of ordinary airplanes, an airfoil is a surface that is wing-shaped. In the context of helicopters, we speak of rotor blades being the machine's airfoils. In either case, it should be noted that there are three basic components to the airfoil: *leading edge, trailing edge*, and *chordline*. The leading edge is the front of the wing or blade; the trailing edge, the rear (sharp) edge of the wing or blade. The chordline is an imaginary line connecting the leading edge and trailing edge, perpendicular to the span axis (Fig. 2-1).

A key feature of airfoils is the fact that the upper and lower surfaces are usually curved. The top surface is almost always convex, while the bottom surface may be convex, flat, or even concave (although concave airfoils are no longer used). It is also common for the top surface to be *more convex* than the bottom surface. Whenever the top surface is more convex than the lower surface, the airfoil is said to have *camber*.

When an airfoil looks the same on either side of the chordline, it is said to be *symmetrical*. Conversely, when the two portions of the airfoil on either side of the chordline differ in profile, even slightly, the airfoil is said to be *asymmetrical* (Fig. 2-2). Most popular airplane airfoils are asymmetrical. (The planes that do not use asymmetrical airfoils are mostly aerobatic aircraft.) Almost all of the common airfoils were invented and catalogued by the NACA (the predecessor of NASA) back in the 1920s and 1930s. Among the most popular airplane airfoils in use today is the NACA 23012. You will find this airfoil on such aircraft as the Cessna 310 and Beech Bonanza, among many others.

Helicopter rotor blades, in contrast to airplane wings, usually have a symmetrical airfoil. The reasons for this are somewhat technical, and involve pitching moments (the tendency for the airfoil to "tuck" or hunt with airspeed variations), and we will not go into the fine points here. Suffice it to say that for good aerodynamic and control reasons (and to make manufacturing somewhat easier

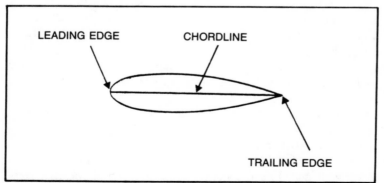

Fig. 2-1. The chordline of an airfoil is an imaginary line joining the leading and trailing edges.

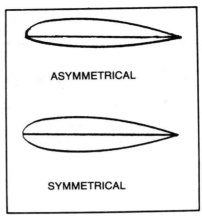

Fig. 2-2. Symmetrical and asymmetrical airfoils.

ASYMMETRICAL

SYMMETRICAL

as well), most helicopter blades have an equal camber on top and bottom surfaces and can thus be characterized by the NACA 0012 notation (where the 12 represents the percentage thickness of the airfoil; i.e., the ratio of the blade's maximum thickness to the chord).

Relative Wind

Before going further, we need to define a few handy terms regarding airfoil flight conditions. In particular, we need to talk about relative wind, angle of incidence (or pitch angle), and angle of attack.

Relative wind is the airflow velocity as "seen" by the airfoil. It is a sort of backwards frame of reference, in that it considers the airfoil itself to be stationary, with only the air moving across it, rather than the reverse (Fig. 2-3). When an airfoil moves forward in the horizontal plane, we say that the relative wind is moving parallel to the airfoil and across the airfoil. If the airfoil moves forward and upward, the relative wind, likewise, is flowing backward and downward.

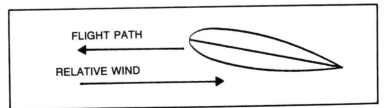

FLIGHT PATH

RELATIVE WIND

Fig. 2-3. Relative wind is always parallel to and in the opposite direction to the flight path of the airfoil.

The important thing to note about relative wind where helicopter rotor blades are concerned is that it can be affected by three factors: the rotation of the blades through the air, the up-and-down flapping movement of the blades, and the horizontal or vertical movement of the whole helicopter through the air. (Talk about a complicated vector problem!)

Pitch angle (or *angle of incidence*) is another term with which you should be familiar. Imagine that the helicopter is on level ground and you are sighting down the length of one blade from the tip. The blade's pitch angle is the angle between the chordline of the airfoil and the horizontal plane of the rotor disc (Fig. 2-4). This angle is important because it can be varied by the pilot (that's you) using the collective pitch control. The cyclic control also effects changes in pitch angle (more on that later). Always remember, however, that the pitch angle is defined in mechanical terms by the relationship of the blade chordline to the pitch linkages on the rotor hub; relative wind can vary in direction and speed without the pitch angle of the blade changing.

Angle of attack is often confused (by novice pilots) with angle of incidence or pitch angle, but they are not the same. Angle of attack can be thought of as the relative wind angle; it is the angle at which the relative wind (wherever it may be coming from) is meeting the chordline of the blade (Fig. 2-5). This is not a mechanically set angle. Nor, if you think about it, is the angle of attack the same at all points on a rotor blade in flight (whereas the pitch

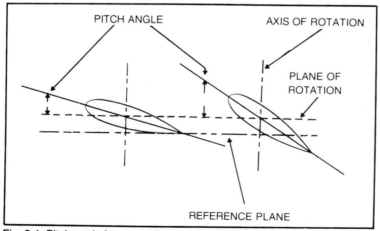

Fig. 2-4. Pitch angle is geometrically defined in relation to the rotor plane or plane of rotation. It is not to be confused with angle of attack.

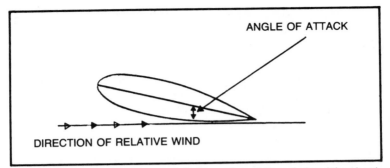

Fig. 2-5. Angle of attack is the angle between the relative wind and the chord-line of the airfoil.

angle *is* the same at all points, unless the blade is twisted). In a hover, in still air, angle of attack and pitch angle will be very nearly the same for all points on all rotor blades, but with any relative wind moving across the helicopter as a whole, or with any cyclic control input from the pilot (see below), angles of attack and pitch angle will no longer be the same.

If you change the pitch angle of the blades (with collective control, say), are you necessarily changing the blades' angle of attack? Yes, because the relative airflow direction has changed with respect to the chordline of the blade. Since this relationship defines angle of attack, the angle has changed.

If your helicopter flies through a momentary updraft, causing a slight change in the effective angle of attack of the rotor blades, has pitch angle changed? No, because pitch angle is a specific geometric relationship between the blade and the rotor hub, which can only be varied by pilot control inputs.

Remember, angle of attack is dependent on relative wind, while pitch angle is dependent on pilot control inputs.

Lift

How, exactly, do all these factors combine to produce lift? Obviously, angle of attack is very important in producing lift, for if a symmetric airfoil is simply faced into the wind at zero angle of attack (chordline parallel to the relative wind), no lift will be produced; while if the angle of attack of that airfoil is gradually increased, a great deal of lift is created.

Other factors are important besides angle of attack, however. (There can even be such a thing as *too much* angle of attack to produce lift. Eventually, as angle of attack is progressively increased, a point is reached where the airflow separates in turbulent fashion from the upper surface of the airfoil, destroying all lift. This is, of course, known as the *stall point*.) Air velocity is also important, since with no air movement, an airfoil can generate no lift. The factors that affect how much lift a given rotor blade or wing will produce include angle of attack, air velocity, air density, airfoil shape (NACA 0012, etc.), and wing or blade surface area. In mathematical terms, the influence of airfoil shape is covered by a term known as *coefficient of lift*, but we will not get into the mathematics of lift here, other than to note that *all* of the above items must be multiplied together to get lift—and air velocity is multiplied by itself (squared), as well. (If air velocity is doubled, lift quadruples.)

How is lift created? Bernoulli's Principle can help explain it. In short, Bernoulli's Principle says merely that if a compressible fluid or gas (such as air) is made to increase in velocity, the pressure of the gas decreases. Anyone who has studied how a carburetor works is familiar with this principle, since it is also known as the *venturi effect*. When a river narrows, the water speeds up until it is past the point of constriction. The same thing happens to air going through a venturi or across a wing. This is the essence of Bernoulli's Principle.

Take a look at an ordinary airplane wing. You'll see that the upper surface is more cambered (more comvex; more curved) than the lower. When a relative wind blows across the airfoil, the air divides; half flows over the top of the wing, while half flows underneath. Both halves must reach the trailing edge at the same time, however, or else a vacuum will be created somewhere. In a crude sense, that's actually what happens—a sort of vacuum *is* created on the upper surface of the wing, because the air—in trying to follow the upper surface—has farther to go than the air on the bottom (less curved) portion of the wing. Essentially, the air flowing across the top of the wing moves at greater speed than the air flowing underneath the wing, and by Bernoulli's Principle, a pressure difference is created which acts to "lift" the wing.

More than that, if you increase the angle of attack of the wing so that the leading edge is higher than the trailing edge, ordinary ram effects will create a high-pressure zone underneath the wing in addition to the Bernoulli-type low-pressure zone above the wing. The net result is a powerful lifting effect. The wing is said to be creating *lift* (Fig. 2-6).

With a helicopter, any control inputs that tend to increase the blades' pitch angle will tend to increase the amount of lift created

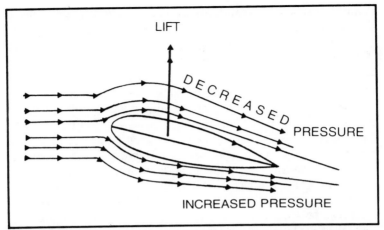

Fig. 2-6. Lift is produced when there is an area of high pressure below the airfoil, combined with an area of low pressure above the airfoil.

by the rotor. (Any control input that tends to increase a single blade's pitch angle will likewise increase just that blade's lift.) Reduction of the pitch angle will similarly *reduce* lift. Changes of rpm will also have an effect on rotor blade lift, obviously. Increase the rpm, and lift goes up; decrease it, and lift decreases.

Air Density

Although it can't be controlled in the same manner as the other factors mentioned above, air density nonetheless plays a very important part in lift generation. *Density*, of course, is defined as the ratio of an object's mass to its volume. You may or may not think of air as an object, but it does have a definite density. The density of air is much greater at sea level than at higher altitudes (falling to about half sea-level density at 18,000 feet). Another way of saying this is that air gets "thinner" the higher you fly. The important thing to note for purposes of our discussion is that it is much more difficult to generate lift in thin (less dense) air than in thick (denser) air.

Air density itself is influenced by several factors—namely temperature, humidity, and pressure. Like most fluids, air expands when it gets hot and contracts when it cools. Therefore, on a hot day air is less dense than on a cool day. The thinness of hot air makes it more difficult to create lift on a hot day (an effect often referred to in the context of *density altitude*). Compounding the problem is the fact that internal combustion engines produce less power in hot, less dense (thin) air than in cold, dense (thick) air. Achieving the power necessary to hover on a hot day is thus often difficult, especially at high-elevation airfields.

Humidity also affects air density, since water molecules in the air are less dense than oxygen or nitrogen molecules (yet take up the same space). Humid air is less dense than dry air, all other factors being equal. Compounding the humidity equation is the fact that hot air is capable of holding much more water vapor than cold air, which means that on a hot day, the pilot often fights the double problem of high humidity and heat-thinned air. The resulting reduced air density makes lift generation more difficult.

Air pressure also has an effect on density. The higher the atmospheric pressure, generally speaking, the thicker the air. This effect can be seen when climbing to altitude; barametric pressure decreases by about one inch of mercury per thousand foot increase in altitude, and density also falls a commensurate amount (i.e., about three percent per thousand feet).

Drag

No airfoil can produce lift without also experiencing *drag*. Like lift, drag is measured in units of force (such as pounds); it is the force that resists the rotor blade's (or wing's) motion through the air. You probably know it as the retarding force of "wind resistance," such as the wind resistance you feel when you stick your hand out of a moving car's window.

Drag is influenced by all the same factors that affect lift: angle of attack, air density, air velocity, airfoil shape, and blade surface area. (And again, air velocity exerts its effect exponentially; drag goes up with the square of airspeed. If you double the blade's airspeed, you'll quadruple the drag force felt by it.) It is the force of drag, acting parallel to but in the opposite direction of the blade's movement, that tends to cause a reduction in rpm when a higher blade pitch angle is selected. Likewise, when a greater rotor rpm is desired, it is necessary to overcome a greater amount of drag; hence, more power is needed.

These effects will become clearer as we go along. For now it's enough to remember that when pitch angle, angle of attack, air density, or air velocity (rotor rpm) are increased, drag automatically increases. It is important to note, however, that when angle of attack is increased, drag does not always increase at the *same rate* as lift. The dynamic variations of lift and drag can be quite complex. Even so, there is usually one angle of attack at which the ratio of lift of drag is at is maximum, and at which lift production is most efficient; helicopter rotor systems are designed to operate at or near this condition at all times.

Stall

When the angle of attack of a blade or wing increases beyond a certain value, air can no longer flow smoothly over the top surface of the airfoil (the required change in direction is too radical). The air instead spills over the leading edge of the blade, creating what's known as a *burble* or area of flow separation. When this condition occurs, lift is destroyed and any further increase in angle of attack only results in increasing drag—not increasing lift. The blade or wing is said to be in a *stalled* condition (Fig. 2-7).

Airplane pilots are very familiar with the concept of stalling, since an airplane's wings stall when the pilot attempts to fly too slow, at too high an angle of attack. Many fixed-wing pilots are under the mistaken belief that stalling is possible only at low speed. Speed *per se* has nothing to do with stalling, however. The key to understanding the stall is *angle of attack*. An airplane's wings can stall at *any* speed, given sufficient angle of attack to induce burble (flow separation).

If you've followed the discussion this far, it should be evident to you that a helicopter's blades can also stall—despite the fact that a rotor blade's tip speed in flight may well be over 300 mph—provided the angle of attack limitations of the airfoil are exceeded. And, as we shall see later, there are indeed times when portions of a helicopter's rotor *are* actually stalling.

When rotor blade stall occurs, lift must be restored by decreas-

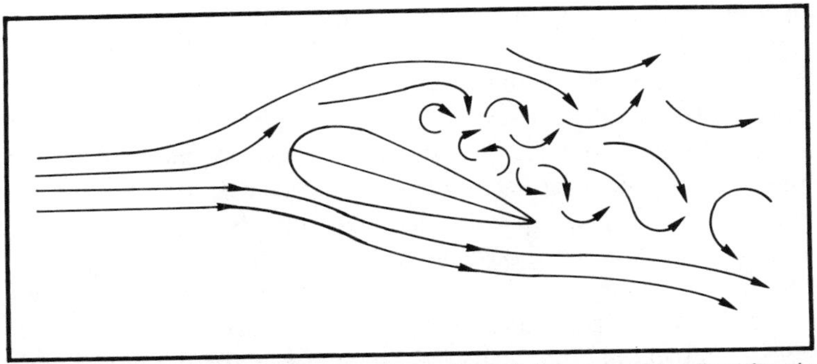

Fig. 2-7. In a stalled condition, the angle of attack is too great to allow the air to "follow" the top surface of the airfoil. As a result, flow separation occurs, lift is destroyed, and drag increases.

ing the angle of attack of the blades. Depending on the condition of flight in which this occurs, it may be appropriate either to increase the rotor rpm (changing the angle of attack indirectly) or reduce the pitch angle of the blades by collective control input. There are times when a change of cyclic control can also alleviate the stalled condition. We will have more to say about blade stall in subsequent chapters.

Weight

The total *weight* of the helicopter (the takeoff or gross weight) is, of course, the primary force that must be overcome by the rotor if flight is to be achieved. Since weight and lift are both measured in pounds, it follows that the amount of lift necessary to hover should equal the weight of the helicopter. This holds true not just for hovering, but for all other steady-state flight conditions (in which the helicopter is changing neither its rate of climb nor its rate of descent). When a climb is initiated, the lift required is more than the weight of the ship; conversely, when the rotor produces less lift than is represented by the weight of the copter, the aircraft enters a descent.

The concept of *center of gravity* is arguably more important to the helicopter pilot than to the fixed-wing pilot, and may be considered more important even than gross weight (since if gross weight is too high, the helicopter will never leave the ground anyway). An object's center of gravity is an imaginary point at which all the mass of the object can essentially be considered to be concentrated, for purposes of mathematical calculations. You can visualize it as the point at which the helicopter would balance on a knife-edge (or actually, *two* knife-edges: one running fore-and-aft, and another running crosswise to the skids).

Why is CG so important? The rotor lifts the helicopter from one point (coincident with the center of the rotor hub), and one point only. If the CG of the helicopter is located directly below that point, then on takeoff the helicopter will lift straight up. But suppose the CG is displaced toward the nose of the copter. Lifting straight up on the rotor hub will result in the helicopter lifting off in a nose-down attitude, and the nose-down "tug" of the CG will cause the machine to want to pitch forward. To counter this, the pilot will have to make a rearward control input on the cyclic (the center stick). But this will not reduce the nose-down attitude of the ship; it will simply arrest the forward motion caused by the initial pitch-down. In the end, the CG of the copter will still be directly below the rotor hub. Unfortunately, a relatively large control input is needed to counter the effects of forward or aft CG problems, and in some helicopters the pilot may run out of cyclic control with a CG that is located as little as *two inches* forward of the ideal center of gravity. If such a helicopter were to lift off, it would pitch over and crash out of control. Hence, it is extremely important to pay attention to CG limits when loading a helicopter, particularly a small helicopter.

The above discussion applies equally to lateral (off center to the side) loadings as to fore-and-aft CG problems. You will notice this when you perform your first solo hover; with the weight of your instructor gone, the helicopter will want to lift off one-skid-low, and some lateral cyclic input will be needed to counteract this effect.

3
Aerodynamics of Helicopter Flight

The basics of lift generation and airfoil behavior were discussed in the preceding chapter. Now let's take a look at what these aerodynamic concepts mean when applied to actual helicopter flight. Along the way we'll explore various facets of rotor-system design that will be important to us later on when we talk about flight controls.

Hovering Flight

Hovering (remaining motionless over a point) can be done either very near the ground or high in the air. The former is known as *hovering in ground effect (HIGE)*; the latter, *hovering out of ground effect (HOGE)*. *Ground effect* refers to the cushion of air that builds between a lifting surface (such as a wing or rotor) and the ground when the aircraft is operating within one rotor diameter (or one wingspan, as appropriate) of ground level. Because of the cushion of air, less power is needed to hover in ground effect than out of ground effect. (Helicopter operating handbooks usually state the HIGE and HOGE ceilings for the aircraft at gross weight. The HOGE ceiling is invariably lower.)

In hovering flight, the *tip path plane* of the rotor is parallel to the ground, and the thrust of the rotor is just equal to the weight of the machine. As explained in the preceding chapter, a climb from hovering flight can only be initiated if total lift exceeds the weight of the ship (Fig. 3-1). This is accomplished by increasing the power delivered to the rotor system. (Some increase of blade pitch angle is also called for.) To descend from a hover, conversely, requires reducing power and/or reducing blade pitch. Note that all of these operations can be (and usually are) done without any changes in rotor rpm.

Forward Flight

To achieve forward flight, it is necessary to incline the tip path plane (or rotor plane) forward slightly (Fig. 3-2). The net effect of this is to tilt the total lift/thrust vector (or force) of the helicopter rotor forward, giving a slight forward component to the rotor's thrust. (Also, since the thrust vector is no longer pointing directly away from the ship's center of gravity, a slight pitch-down of the nose of the aircraft will take place.) The forward component of the rotor's thrust will cause the helicopter to accelerate forward until the total drag on the helicopter equals the forward thrust component. At that point, the forward speed of the ship will remain constant, until or unless a further inclination of the rotor disc is brought about by additional control inputs.

Note that when the thrust vector is inclined forward, the vertical lift component is no longer what it was in hovering flight; some lift has been lost by the mere act of angling the rotor forward. The helicopter, as a result, will want to settle unless the pilot acts to "make up" the lost lift by adding an increment of power and/or collective pitch. (As we will see shortly, power and pitch are usually applied simultaneously.) The further forward the rotor is tilted, the more power/pitch must be added to make up for the lost lift.

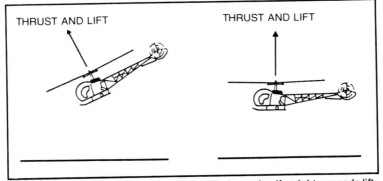

Fig. 3-1. When total lift exceeds weight, a climb results; if weight exceeds lift, a descent occurs.

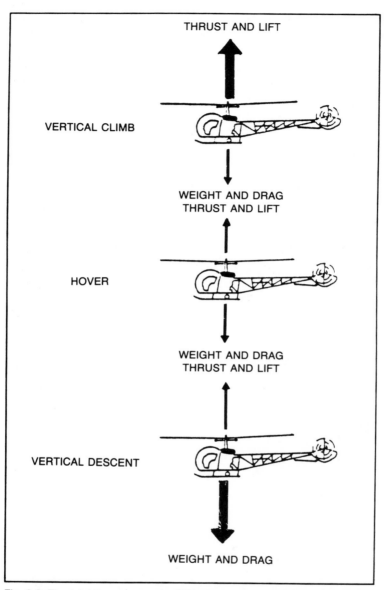

Fig. 3-2. The total thrust vector (or lifting force) of the rotor always acts perpendicular to the rotor disc or tip path plane.

Translational Lift

Once the helicopter has attained a forward airspeed of approximately 25 mph or more, the rotor disc begins to acquire the properties of a gigantic circular wing, in that onrushing air begins to flow over and below the rotor disc in a manner similar to the airflow around a wing. The result is a dramatic increase in overall lift not accompanied by an increase in required power. This sudden bonus of lift due to air flowing over and under the rotor at speeds of 25 mph or more is referred to as *translational lift* and is a very important consideration in helicopter operations. For now, it's merely important to know that such a phenomenon exists and can be counted on to occur any time the rotor is experiencing a relative wind of 25 mph or more. In other words, it is actual airspeed—not ground speed—that makes translational lift possible. In a stiff wind (of 25 mph or more), a helicopter can and will experience translational lift even in a hover, with no forward speed at all (relative to the ground).

At first, it may seem paradoxical that *less* power is needed to operate a helicopter in forward flight than in a hover, but this is precisely the case. It is also the case that hovering out of ground effect requires the most power of any helicopter flight regime—a fact that will be worth remembering throughout later phases of this book.

Sideward and Rearward Flight

Helicopters can, of course, fly in any direction. By easing the center control stick (the cyclic) in the direction the pilot wishes to go, the pilot can cause the rotor thrust vector to incline in that direction, producing a thrust component that will carry the helicopter in that direction (Fig. 3-3). It is important to note that most of the rotor's thrust is still needed to counteract the force of gravity, and the actual angle of inclination of the rotor during sideward or rearward flight will be so small as to be imperceptible to the eye of an observer. You have no doubt noticed that even in cruise flight, a helicopter's rotor is barely inclined forward.

As in translational (forward) flight, tilting the rotor disc in a sideward or rearward direction causes a slight reduction in available vertical thrust component, since some of the helicopter's original thrust is being used to generate a side thrust component. The net result is that the helicopter will begin to sink slightly as the rotor is inclined to one side, unless additional power is added. Also, as speed is picked up in any direction, the whole helicopter tends to want to slide off its cushion of air, and in exiting the HIGE condition, even more power will be needed to keep from settling.

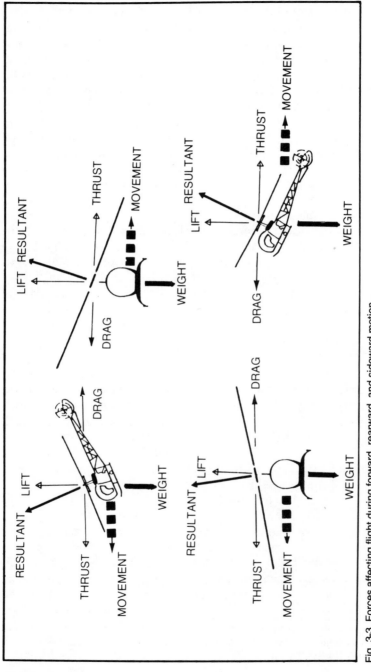

Fig. 3-3. Forces affecting flight during forward, rearward, and sideward motion.

Torque Counteraction

So far, our discussion of helicopter aerodynamics has taken in the relatively simple subjects of lift (thrust) and drag, and applied them to hovering and translational flight, but we have not yet said anything about directional control. As you know from reading Chapter 1, a recurring theme in the history of helicopter development is the search for adequate means of control. Merely coupling enough horsepower to a rotor or set of rotors to achieve vertical flight is not difficult at all; Louis Breguet accomplished this before World War I. The difficult part of designing a successful helicopter is making it *controllable*.

The problem is that a helicopter has more degrees of freedom of motion than an airplane, yet (unlike an airplane) has no inherent, built-in stability. With a helicopter, you can go up or down vertically, move forward or aft, travel sideways; *bank* sideways (as in a coordinated turn); and/or rotate or *yaw* from side to side (nose left or nose right). In a hover, the slightest wind gust or perturbation can set in motion a change of the helicopter's direction, attitude, or altitude, and since the machine has no inherent stability, the perturbation will only continue to exert its effect, spinning the helicopter or sending it sideways, up, or down, until the pilot counteracts the effect with a deliberate control input.

In a single-rotor helicopter, directional control is more complicated than it seems, thanks to the effects of main-rotor *torque*. By Newton's Third Law, we know that for every action there is an equal but opposite reaction; applied to helicopters, this means that

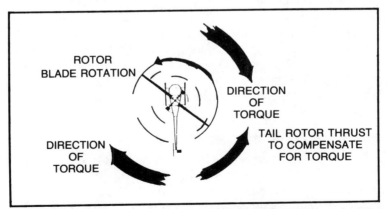

Fig. 3-4. Tail rotor thrust compensates for the torque effect of the main rotor, which would otherwise spin the helicopter fuselage in the opposite direction to the main rotor.

whenever an attempt is made to turn a rotor in one direction, the object doing the turning (i.e., the engine and everything attached to it) will want to turn in the opposite direction. We call this turning tendency *torque*.

Even the earliest of helicopter inventors knew that some means would have to be provided to counteract rotor torque to keep the entire aircraft from spinning around wildly. That's why many of the first rotorcraft were of the twin counterrotating rotors variety. When you turn two rotors in opposite directions, the torque from one rotor exactly cancels or counteracts the torque from the other. (Yaw control is then a simple matter of individually varying the drag or thrust produced by the rotors.)

In a single-rotor helicopter, torque is counteracted by means of a small tail rotor at the end of a fuselage boom, mounted in a vertical plane so as to produce a sideways thrust. In every conventional helicopter without exception, this small tail rotor (or *antitorque rotor*, as it is more properly called) is driven by a reduction drive off the main rotor transmission. In other words, the tail rotor always turns when the main rotor turns; moreover, the rpm ratio between the main rotor and tail rotor is fixed, and you cannot vary one without varying the other (Fig. 3-4).

The pilot has control over the tail rotor's thrust, but not in the sense of controlling its rpm. Rather than vary thrust by changing rpm, the pilot varies the tail rotor's thrust by changing the pitch angle of the tail rotor's blades. This is accomplished mechanically through rudder pedals (or, more properly, *anti-torque pedals*) on the cockpit floor, which are connected via cables and/or push-pull tubes to the pitch linkages on the tail rotor blades at the rear of the ship.

Note: Because of material limitations on gearboxes, moving a copter's main rotor by hand (on the ground, before startup) is generally okay, but attempting to spin the tail rotor by hand is *strictly forbidden*. When it is necessary to check tail rotor motion on the ground, do so by rotating the ship's main rotor; never turn the tail rotor by hand.

Forces Acting on the Main Rotor Blades

In order to fully appreciate how a control input results in a given aerodynamic effect, it is essential that you acquaint yourself with the forces at work on the rotor blade in flight, and the ramifications of these forces for control-system design. The principle forces of interest to us are as follows.

Flapping: In forward flight, or any time a relative wind is present for the helicopter as a whole, an asymmetric lift condition develops across the rotor disc due to the fact that the advancing blades (those blades traveling into the relative wind) are developing more lift than the retreating blades (those blades traveling downwind). In normal cruise flight, a small helicopter's rotor blades may be operating at 400 rpm, traveling with a tip speed of 450 mph. In forward flight at 50 mph, the advancing blades will have a tip speed of 450 plus 50, or 500 mph. But the same blades, when they reach the retreating side of the disc, will have an effective tip speed of just 450 minus 50, or 400 mph—a difference of 100 mph from one side of the rotor to the other! Since lift varies with the square of airspeed, this means a very substantial difference in lift between the advancing and retreating blades. Were nothing to be done about it, the helicopter would roll over to one side uncontrollably.

To keep this from happening, rotor blades are attached to the hub by means of a horizontal hinge pin which allows the blades to flap up and down freely as they rotate. What actually happens in forward flight is that the advancing blade, of its own accord, dissipates its extra lift by flapping upward. (The blade's upward movement results in a *decrease* in effective angle of attack, because the relative wind changes from a horizontal direction to a more downward direction as the blade is moving up.) On the retreating side, the blade, reacting to the loss of airspeed (and attendant loss of lift), flaps *downward*, which causes an *increase* in the blade's effective angle of attack (Fig. 3-5). The combination of decreased angle of attack on the advancing blades plus increased angle of attack on the retreating blades tends to equalize the lift over the two halves of the rotor disc. (*Note:* In a two-bladed, teetering rotor system such as the one used on the Bell 47, the blades flap as a unit. The net result is still the same, however.)

Coning: Because they are free to flap, a helicopter's rotor blades tend to seek their own vertical position in flight based on the weight of the ship (which tends of course to pull down on the center of the disc, increasing the overall flapping angle of the blades much as a tightrope walker causes a depression in the center of his rope) and centrifugal forces (which tend to keep the blades straight out perpendicular). Centrifugal force is far and away the most significant force acting on the rotor blades. Even a lightweight blade weighing no more than 30 pounds exerts *tons* of centrifugal force on the rotor hub in flight. But great as the centrifugal force may be, the rotor blades still do not fly exactly straight out from the hub; instead, there is always some small *coning angle*. In a two-

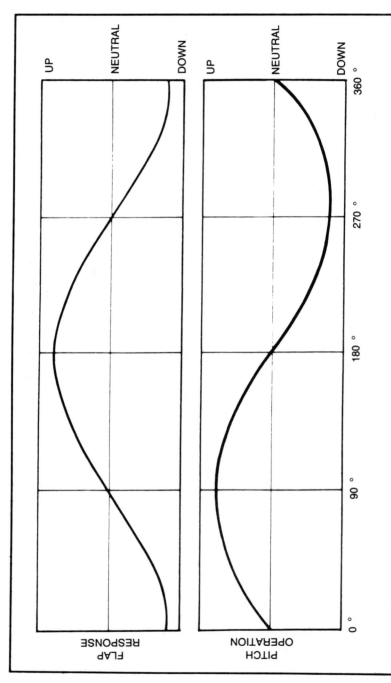

44

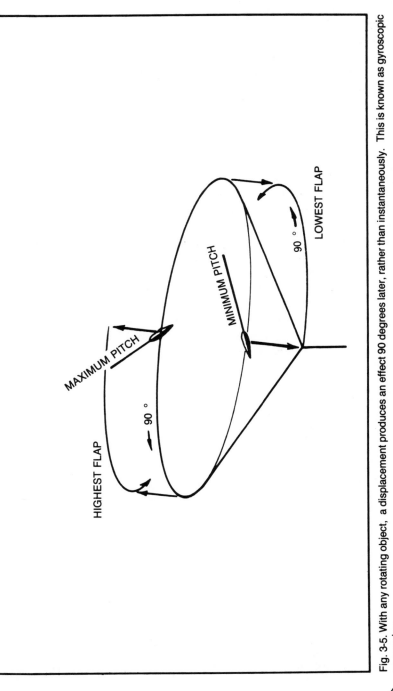

Fig. 3-5. With any rotating object, a displacement produces an effect 90 degrees later, rather than instantaneously. This is known as gyroscopic precession.

bladed, teetering rotor system (Bell 47, Hiller UH-12), a coning angle is built into the hub, since otherwise the angle would have to be achieved by blade bending. The coning angle actually sought by the blades will vary in flight, of course, depending on gross weight, rotor rpm, and G-forces developed in maneuvers (Fig. 3-6).

Coriolis effect: You have no doubt noticed how, when an ice skater pulls her arms in to her chest during a pirouette, her rotational speed increases dramatically (through conservation of angular momentum). A similar situation occurs when a rotor blade flaps upward, in effect bringing its center of gravity more toward the axis of rotation of the rotor. The result is that the upward-flapping blade tends to want to speed up. Of course, it can't do that if the other blades do not also want to speed up. Still, significant fore-and-aft bending forces are generated by the tendency of up- and down-flapping blades to speed up or slow down. This lead/lag tendency is usually given the name *Coriolis effect* (Fig. 3-7).

To relieve the stresses involved in Coriolis bending (which might otherwise culminate in fatigue damage to the blade attachment, or the blade itself), helicopter designers usually incorporate a *lead-lag hinge* (i.e., a vertical hinge pin) in the blade attachment, or even midway out on the blade itself (Brantly B-2B), along with a viscous damper to help dampen out vibrations caused by blade "hunting" in the plane of rotation. Two-bladed rotor systems aren't

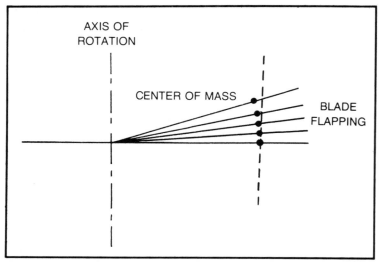

Fig. 3-6. The "axis of rotation" is an imaginary line, perpendicular to the tip path plane, around which the rotor turns. Thrust acts vertically along this line.

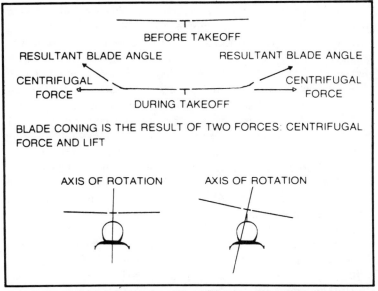

BEFORE TAKEOFF

RESULTANT BLADE ANGLE   RESULTANT BLADE ANGLE

CENTRIFUGAL   CENTRIFUGAL
FORCE   FORCE

DURING TAKEOFF

BLADE CONING IS THE RESULT OF TWO FORCES: CENTRIFUGAL
FORCE AND LIFT

AXIS OF ROTATION   AXIS OF ROTATION

Fig. 3-7. When a blade flaps upward, its center of gravity shifts inward, toward the center of the hub, and (like an ice skater bringing her arms closer to her body) the blade wants to speed up. This is otherwise known as Coriolis effect.

affected by Coriolis factors to the same degree as three- and four-bladed systems, and conventional lead-lag (or drag) hinges aren't usually employed on the blades, but the teetering hub is usually underslung (hung on a spanwise pivot) to keep the center of mass of the rotor system as a whole very nearly constant in location even as the blades bend and flex.

Precession: The spinning blades of the helicopter rotor, because they are free to flap (and lead and lag), do not impart much gyroscopic stability to the helicopter itself. The blades are, however, subject to the effects of *gyroscopic precession*, which is the phenomenon wherein a rotating object, given an externally applied force, reacts to the force 90 degrees of rotation beyond the point of initial disturbance. What it means for a helicopter whose rotor spins counterclockwise when viewed from above (as is the case with all U. S. production helicopters) is that an increase in pitch angle of one blade, if begun when the blade is at three o'clock to the helicopter cockpit, will not cause the blade to flap upward until it has reached the 12 o'clock position. In purely mechanical terms, this effect is not hard to deal with at all, since one can easily design the control system so that cyclic variations of pitch can be inputted 90 degrees out of phase with the intended direction of helicopter travel so as to give the pilot a totally natural-feeling control stick (from a push-forward/go-forward point of view). However, some control lag inevitably occurs, and as a result the stick action is rarely as fast in a light, three-bladed helicopter as it is in a light airplane. Also, because the helicopter's rotor blades are free to seek their own flapping and lead-lag equilibrium position in flight (due to the many hinge points on the rotor hub), aerodynamic feedback from the blades to the control stick (cyclic) is virtually nil. The pilot feels mainly the friction and inertia of the control-system pull-tubes.

You'll note that because of the phenomenon of precession (or *phase lag*, as it is sometimes called), the blade flapping that occurs in forward flight due to dissymmetry of lift does not occur at the sides of the ship, but at a fore and aft position. The advancing blade reaches its maximum point of upward flapping at the ship's 12 o'clock position, while the retreating blade reaches its maximum downward flapping at the rear of the copter. The actual amount of flapping involved is not great, in any case (in fact, it is too small for the untrained eye to notice).

Transverse Airflow

Transverse airflow—not to be confused with *translational lift* (see above)—is a condition that affects the main rotor any time the helicopter is in forward flight; it is an airflow anomaly wherein the rear portion of the rotor arc has a higher downwash velocity than the front portion. This increased downwash speed is caused by the fact that air passing through the rear portion of the rotor disc has been accelerated for a longer time than air passing through the forwardmost portion. In other words, the relative wind is of a slightly greater magnitude at the rear than at the front. The net effect is to cause greater lift to be created at the rear edge of the rotor disc, and by normal precession, this extra lift results in the rotor blades riding higher 90 degrees later (on the starboard side of the rotor, in an American-made helicopter), which in turn causes an effective lateral displacement of the thrust vector to the left. To put it differently, the net effect of transverse flow (the difference in acceleration of air through the front and rear portions of the rotor disc) is to cause the rotor tip path plane to incline to the left slightly in forward flight. The faster the helicopter's cruise speed, the greater the transverse flow and the more the helicopter wants to bank to the left.

You will notice the effects of transverse lift as you make the transition from high cruise to low-speed letdown and hover. As the helicopter's airspeed bleeds off, you will find that the "neutral" position of the cyclic control will seem to shift more and more to the left, until in hover you are holding the stick well to the left of the position that gave neutral bank in cruise. (Another occasion on which you will notice transverse flow is on entry into translational lift, where it can be accompanied by vibration.)

Yaw Control

Yaw control, as discussed above under "Torque Counteraction," is effected in the cockpit by foot pedal action, which results in changes in tail rotor thrust. By pressing the left pedal, the pilot can make the nose of the helicopter swing to the left. By pressing the right pedal, the nose can be made to swing to the right.

In theory, yaw control is easy; in practice, it is more challenging (especially for beginning helicopter pilots) than it at first looks. Remember, the foot pedals are not just for establishing a heading, but are for torque counteraction, which is a much more dynamic state of affairs than the average non-helicopter-pilot realizes.

Any time the power to the main rotor increases or decreases, torque increases or decreases and a new pedal position is called for. Maximum power is generally used in hover (especially HOGE) and/or a maximum-rate climb; under these conditions, torque is at a maximum and in an American-built helicopter with main rotor turning counterclockwise (viewed from above), a large amount of left pedal displacement is needed to keep the helicopter from yawing to the right (i.e., rotating clockwise). In forward flight—after translational lift has been attained—less power is needed than in a hover; also, aerodynamic forces acting on the tail in cruise tend to keep the helicopter tracking nose-straight-ahead. Accordingly, much less left pedal pressure is needed in forward flight. (In fact, most helicopters are rigged to have anti-torque pedals neutral for cruise flight.)

In a descent, with very little power being transmitted to the main rotor, little torque counteraction is called for, and (in a U. S.-built helicopter) some right pedal pressure may be needed to trim the ship for the *lack* of torque. Moreover, in a power-off descent (or *autorotation*, as it's called), friction forces at the rotor shaft will actually cause the helicopter to want to turn *in the same direction as* the rotor, and a very significant amount of right-pedal pressure will be needed to keep the helicopter tracking nose-straight-ahead. Of course, any subsequent addition of power will make the ship's nose want to turn opposite the rotor, and left pedal deflection will be needed.

Tail Rotor Drift

As you would expect, since the tail rotor is acting as a sideways-thrusting propeller, the entire helicopter has a tendency to move in the direction of tail rotor thrust in a hover (Fig. 3-8). In a U. S. helicopter, this would be a tendency to drift to the right. This movement is often referred to as *translating tendency* or *tail rotor drift*. To counteract this drifting tendency, the rotor mast in some helicopters is actually rigged to incline slightly to one side (the left side, in American-built copters) so as to give the rotor thrust vector a built-in bias to the left. In other helicopters, the cyclic pitch control system may be rigged in such a way as to bias the tip path plane to the left even though the rotor mast is straight up and down. Even so, most helicopters tend to hover with one skid lower to the ground than the other. Tail rotor thrust is the reason.

Pendular Action

Since the fuselage of the helicopter is suspended from a single

Fig. 3-8. The tail rotor turns at a fixed multiple of main-rotor rpm. It produces a significant side-thrust which makes the helicopter want to move sideways (drift) unless opposite cyclic is applied.

50

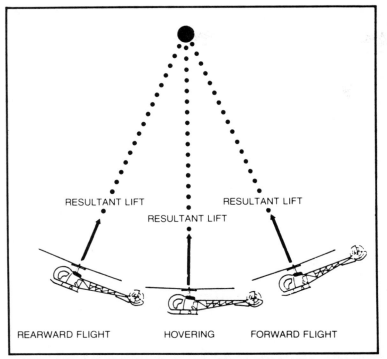

RESULTANT LIFT

RESULTANT LIFT

RESULTANT LIFT

REARWARD FLIGHT   HOVERING   FORWARD FLIGHT

Fig. 3-9. A helicopter acts much like a pendulum suspended from the rotor head. Turbulence can cause the pendulum action to begin. The pilot should not "fight" this pendulum action, but should neutralize the cyclic.

point and has considerable mass, it acts much like a ball suspended from a string in flight (Fig. 3-9). It is free to oscillate laterally (side to side) or longitudinally (fore and aft) in flight, like a pendulum, and a slight wind gust or pocket of turbulence may be all that's needed to induce this oscillation. The pendular action is self-dampening, however, and generally speaking the pilot should not be overly concerned with counteracting the movement with cyclic control inputs, since such inputs often have a way of exaggerating the original perturbation. Beginning helicopter pilots are well-advised to *hold the cyclic control motionless* upon encountering any pendular action. To do otherwise is to risk upsetting the craft even further.

4
Flight Controls

There are basically four controls in a helicopter that you use during flight: cyclic pitch, collective pitch, throttle and antitorque (Fig. 4-1).

With the use of these four controls, you can lift off, hover, transition, fly to your destination, and land. By taking a look at their individual roles, as well as their integration into the total systems, helicopter flight concepts can better be understood.

Collective Pitch Control

The collective pitch lever, simply called the *collective*, is located on the left side of the pilot's seat in most models and is operated by the pilot's left hand. The collective moves up and down, pivoting at the rear and, through a series of mechanical linkages, changing the pitch angle of the main rotor blades simultaneously (Fig. 4-2).

As collective is raised, there's a simultaneous, and equal, increase in the pitch angle of all the main rotor blades. And, as it's lowered, there's a simultaneous, and equal, decrease in main rotor blades pitch angle. The amount of lever movement determines the extent of pitch angle change.

As the rotor blades' pitch angle changes, the angle of attack of each blade will also change. This change in the angle of attack will affect the blade's lift characteristics. As the angle of attack increases, drag and lift increase; however, rotor rpm decreases. As

Fig. 4-1. The helicopter pilots' primary flight controls are the antitorque (rudder) pedals, center stick or cyclic, and collective control (not visible) to the left of the pilot's seat. At the end of the collective is a twist-grip throttle. This Robinson R-22 is well-equipped by small chopper standards, with full gyro panel, navcom, DME, and ADF.

the angle of attack decreases, lift and drag decrease, but rotor rpm increases.

Since it's essential that rotor rpm remain constant, there must be some means of making a proportionate change in the power to compensate for the change in drag/rpm. This coordination of power with blade pitch angle is usually controlled through a special cam linkage which automatically increases power when the collective is raised and decreases power when the collective is lowered. This feature is known as *correlation*.

The collective is the *primary* altitude control. Raising the collective increases the rotor's lift and, through the cam linkage with the throttle, increases engine power. The collective controls rotor rpm; the throttle controls manifold pressure.

Throttle Control

The throttle, often thought of as synonomous with the collective, is mounted on the forward end of the collective lever in the form of a twist-type grip on most helicopter models. The primary function of the throttle is to regulate rotor rpm directly and engine rpm indirectly.

In many smaller choppers there isn't any automatic syncronization of collective and rpm, in which case it has to be done manually by twisting the throttle grip. Also, you may want to adjust or fine tune the rpm. Twisting the motorcycle-type grip outboard will increase rpm, and twisting inboard will decrease rpm.

Used properly, the collective and throttle attachment work together, giving you the right blade pitch angle, manifold pressure (power) and rotor rpm. Since the collective is considered the primary control for rotor speed and the throttle is considered the primary control for manifold pressure, they must work harmoniously together.

Remember, the collective also influences manifold pressure and the throttle also influences rotor rpm; each is considered to be a secondary control for each other's function. You must analyze both the tachometer (rpm indicator) as well as the manifold pressure gauge, which are usually housed in the same unit for convenience. As a simplification, take a look at some sample problems that are common with this system and their solutions:

Problem: Manifold pressure low, rotor rpm low.

Solution: Increasing throttle will increase manifold pressure, and a higher rotor rpm will result.

Problem: Manifold pressure high, rotor rpm low.

Solution: Decreasing collective will reduce manifold pressure, decrease drag on the rotor, and a higher rpm will result.

Fig. 4-2. The Robinson R-22 rotor head is of the two-bladed, teetering type. Note the blade pitch links, which connect at the bottom to a standard swash-plate assembly. All cyclic and collective pitch changes occur through the action of those two pitch links.

Problem: Manifold pressure high, rotor rpm high.

Solution: Decreasing throttle reduces manifold pressure and results in a reduction of rotor rpm.

Problem: Manifold pressure low, rotor rpm high.

Solution: Increasing collective will increase manifold pressure, increase rotor drag, and a lower rotor rpm will result.

Flying a helicopter has often been compared to flying a heavy airplane at slow speeds. It takes time for corrections to be made—time between input of corrective measures on the controls and the time to helicopter response. It could possibly take as much as two seconds or more for the craft to respond to control input. This is one reason to avoid large adjustments. All corrections need to be accomplished through smooth pressure on the controls. Don't get anxious at not having a quick response and increase the input or put in another correction altogether. You'll end up "chasing the needles."

Antitorque (Rudder) Pedals

Thrust produced by the auxiliary (tail) rotor is governed by the position of the *antitorque pedals*. These pedals are linked to a pitch change mechanism in the tail rotor gearbox and permit the pilot to increase or decrease the pitch of the tail rotor blades. The primary purpose of the tail rotor and its controls is to counteract the torque effect of the main rotor (Fig. 4-3).

The tail rotor and its controls not only enable you to counteract the torque of the main rotor, but also to control the heading of the helicopter during a hover, hovering turns and hovering patterns. Understand that in forward flight, the rudder pedals are not used to control the heading of the craft, except during portions of crosswind takeoffs and approaches. They are, rather, used to compensate for torque—to put the helicopter in longitudinal trim so that coordination can be maintained. The cyclic control is used to change heading by making a coordinated turn to the desired direction.

For being so relatively simple, the development of an antitorque device puzzled the masters for many years. In any case, it takes no genius to understand the simplicity with which it works.

With the right pedal moved forward, the tail rotor's blades either have a negative pitch angle or a small positive pitch angle. The farther forward the right pedal is pushed, the larger the negative pitch angle. The nearer the right pedal is to the neutral position, the more positive pitch angle and tail rotor will have. Somewhere in between, the tail rotor will have a zero pitch angle. As the left pedal is moved forward of the neutral position, the positive pitch angle of the tail rotor increases, until it becomes maximum with full forward displacement of the left pedal.

With a negative pitch angle, the tail rotor thrust is working in the same direction as torque reaction of the main rotor, and with a small positive pitch angle, the tail rotor doesn't produce enough thrust to overcome the torque effect of the main rotor during cruising flight. Therefore, if the right pedal is displaced forward of neutral during cruising flight, the tail rotor thrust will not overcome the torque effect, and the nose will yaw to the right.

The tail rotor will usually have a medium, positive pitch angle with the pedals in the neutral position. In the medium positive pitch, the tail rotor thrust approximately equals the torque of the main rotor during cruising flight, so the helicopter is rigged to maintain a constant heading in level cruise flight.

With the left pedal in forward position, the tail rotor is in a high positive pitch position. In a high positive pitch position, tail rotor thrust exceeds that needed to overcome torque effect during cruising flight, so the helicopter's nose will yaw to the left.

This explanation is based on cruising power and airspeed. Since

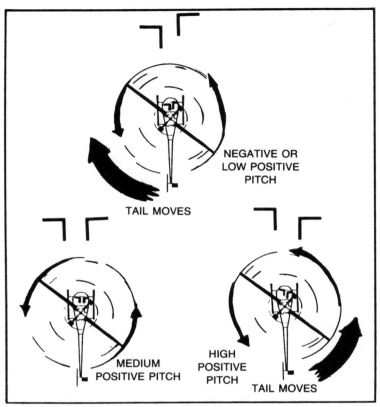

Fig. 4-3. Pedal position in relation to tail rotor thrust.

the amount of torque is dependent on the amount of engine power being supplied to the main rotor, the relative position of the pedals required to counteract torque will depend on the amount of power being used at any time. In general, the less power being used, the greater the forward displacement of the right pedal; the greater the power being used, the greater the forward displacement of the left pedal.

The maximum positive pitch angle of the tail rotor is generally greater than the maximum negative pitch angle available. This is because the primary purpose of the tail rotor is to counteract the torque of the main rotor. The capability for tail rotors to produce thrust to the left (negative pitch angle) is necessary, because during autorotation, the drag of the transmission tends to yaw the nose to the left in the same direction that the main rotor is turning.

It should be noted that in French (and Soviet, and some

homebuilt) helicopters, the main rotor turns exactly opposite the direction of U. S. civil helicopters (Fig. 4-4). Such helicopters are flown with a slight forward displacement of the *right* pedal in a hover, accordingly, with *left* pedal used in power-off descents.

Cyclic Pitch Control

As discussed earlier, the at rest lift/thrust force is always perpendicular to the tip-path plane of the main rotor. When the tip-path plane is tilted away from the horizontal, the lift/thrust force is divided into two components: horizontal thrust and vertical lift. The purpose of the *cyclic pitch control* (cyclic) is to tilt the tip-path plane in the direction that horizontal movement is desired. The thrust component then pulls the helicopter in the direction of rotor tilt. The cyclic control has no effect on the *magnitude* of the total lift/thrust force, but merely changes the *direction* of this force, thus controlling the attitude and airspeed of the ship (Figs. 4-5, 4-6).

It sounds simple, because it is simple. The rotor disc tilts in the direction that pressure is applied to the cyclic. The rotor disc follows the input on the cyclic. If the cyclic is moved forward, the rotor disc tilts forward; if the cyclic is moved aft, the rotor disc tilts aft, and so on.

Fig. 4-4. The Augusta 109A has a conventional-turning (counterclockwise from above) rotor, but not all foreign-made helicopters do. Many foreign ships have clockwise-turning rotors, which means the pilot must be ready to counteract torque with rudder inputs opposite what he learned in training.

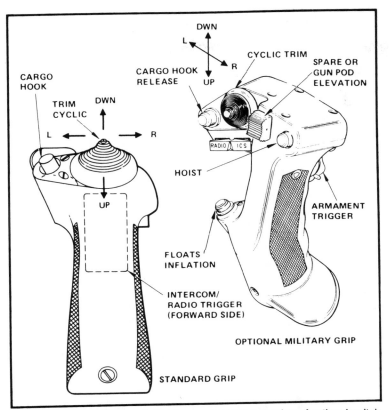

Fig. 4-5. The cyclic (center stick) grip may combine a number of optional switch functions.

So that the rotor disc will always tilt in the direction the cyclic is displaced, the mechanical linkage between the cyclic and the rotor, through the *swashplate*, must be such that the maximum downward deflection of the blades is reached in the direction the stick is displaced; the maximum upward deflection is reached in the opposite direction. In actual practice, this means pitch changes must be initiated 90 degrees before the desired point of blade reaction.

Remember, it was earlier stated, that 90 degrees of phase lag occurs between input and reaction, due to forces of precession. It also applies in this instance. Through mechanical linkage, pitch angle is altered 90 degrees before the blades reach the direction of displacement of the cyclic. As an example, as the cyclic stick is displaced forward, the angle of attack is decreased as the rotor

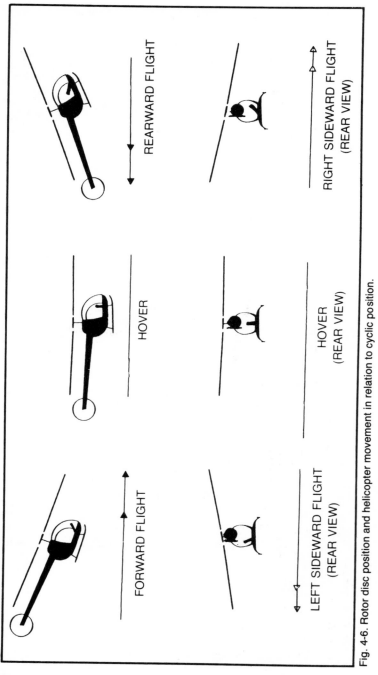

REARWARD FLIGHT

RIGHT SIDEWARD FLIGHT
(REAR VIEW)

HOVER

HOVER
(REAR VIEW)

FORWARD FLIGHT

LEFT SIDEWARD FLIGHT
(REAR VIEW)

Fig. 4-6. Rotor disc position and helicopter movement in relation to cyclic position.

blades pass the 90 degree position to the pilot's right and increases as the blades pass the 90 degree position to the pilot's left. Because of gyroscopic precession, maximum downward deflection of the rotor blades is forward, and maximum upward deflection is aft, causing the rotor disc to tilt forward in the same direction as cyclic displacement. A similar analysis could be made for any direction of displacement of the cyclic.

Note that when we say the rotor disc is "tilted" in a particular direction, we do not mean that the rotor mast actually tilts; what really happens is that the pitch angle of each blade is varied cyclically during its travel around the rotor disc in such a way as to make the blade take the desired flight path to effectively incline the tip-path plane. This is why the cyclic is called the cyclic: It produces cyclic variations in blade pitch. The rotor mast (or driveshaft) never actually tilts. The disc tilts in relation to the shaft, however, and this is what gives the pilot the necessary control over the helicopter's thrust vector.

5
Systems and Components

In preceding chapters, we've discussed basic aerodynamics, the aerodynamics of flight, and flight controls. In this chapter, some of the helicopter's other systems and components and their functions will be discussed to help familiarize you with the overall craft (Fig. 5-1).

Transmission System

The *transmission* does just what its name implies: It transmits engine power to the main rotor, tail rotor, generator, and other accessories. In a sense, it's what makes the machine go (Fig. 5-2).

The engine must operate at a relatively high speed, while the main rotor turns at a much lower rpm. This speed reduction is accomplished through reduction gears in the transmission system.

A helicopter's reduction system is generally somewhere between 6:1 and 9:1. This simply means that, depending on which ratio is used, for every six to nine engine revolutions, the blades rotate one time. Using these ratios, it's easy to see that if the engine turns at 2700 rpm, for instance, the main rotor would turn up at 450 rpm at a 6:1 ratio and 300 rpm at a 9:1 reduction.

When the rotor tachometer needle and the engine tachometer needle are superimposed over each other in the same instrument unit, the ratio of the engine rpm to the rotor rpm is the same as the gear reduction ratio. This single instrument unit, housing both

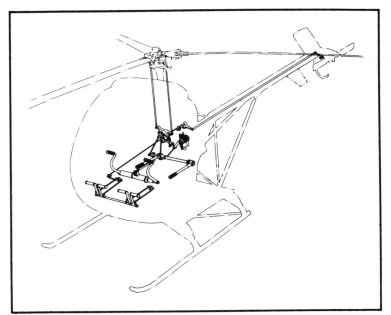

Fig. 5-1. The Hughes 269A control system is typical of many small helicopters' in that it uses simple push-pull tubes and cables, without hydraulic assist.

Fig. 5-2. The Robinson R-22's engine is partly exposed in flight. Transmission is accessed through cowl panels above the engine.

engine and rotor rpm, makes for simple visual interpretation and does away with superfluous instrument clutter.

Clutch

It's standard practice in the conventional, fixed-wing airplane to have the engine and the propeller permanently connected. Since the prop serves as a flywheel, there's no reason for the propeller to be at a standstill while the engine is running. With the helicopter, however, there's a different relationship between the engine and the rotor.

Since the helicopter's rotor weighs so much more than the prop of an airplane, it's necessary to have the rotor disconnect from the engine during start and warmup to relieve the load. Even more important, there must be some way to disconnect the engine from the rotor in case of engine seizure, since otherwise the rotor might slow dangerously. It is, therefore, necessary to have a clutch between the engine and the rotor. Usually, there is an overrunning clutch as well as an idler clutch.

The clutch assembly allows the engine to be started and gradually assume the load of driving the heavy rotor system.

Some helicopters use a centrifugal clutch, in which contact between the inner and outer parts is made by spring-loaded clutch shoes. The inner portion of the clutch (the shoes) is rotated by the engine. The outer portion of the clutch (the drum) is connected to the main rotor through the tramsmission.

At low engine speeds, the clutch shoes are held out of contact with the clutch drum by the springs. As the engine speeds up, centrifugal force throws the clutch shoes outward until they contact the clutch drum. Motion is thus transmitted from the engine driveshaft to the input driveshaft of the transmission. The rotor starts to turn, slowly at first, but increases speed as friction develops sufficiently to drive the drum at engine rpm.

As the clutch becomes fully engaged, the rotor system is driven at the equivalent of engine rpm, and the rotor tachometer needle and engine tachometer needle join or "marry," one needle superimposed over the other.

The rotor rpm equivalent to the engine rpm depends upon the gear reduction ratio between the engine and rotor system for that particular helicopter.

The friction of idler system clutch is manually engaged by the pilot through a lever in the cockpit. Power from the engine driveshaft is transmitted to the transmission driveshaft by a series of friction discs or belts. With this type of clutch, it's possible to start the engine and warm it up without engaging the rotors.

Freewheeling Unit

As previously discussed, in normal operation the rotor system slowly engages and keeps up with engine rpm. When the engine slows below the equivalent of rotor rpm or stops altogether, a freewheeling unit or coupling automatically disconnects the rotor system from the engine. When the engine is disconnected from the rotor system through the automatic action of the freewheeling coupling, the tachometer needles split and the transmission continues to rotate with the main rotor, thereby enabling the tail rotor to continue turning at its normal rate. This is important, because it allows the pilot to maintain directional control during autorotation.

Swashplate Assembly

The swashplate (the mechanism through which cyclic control action occurs) consists of two primary elements through which the rotor mast passes: *stationary star* and *rotating star*.

The stationary star is a disc linked to the cyclic pitch control. The disc is capable of tilting in any direction, but it doesn't rotate as the rotor turns. This non-rotating disc is attached by a bearing surface to a second disc, the rotating star, which turns with the rotor and is mechanically linked to the rotor blade pitch horns.

The rotor blade pitch horns are placed approximately 90 degrees ahead of, or behind, the blade on which they control the pitch change. If this were not done, gyroscopic precession would cause the movement of the craft to be 90 degrees out of phase with the movement of the cyclic pitch stick. As an example, if the cyclic stick were moved to the right, the helicopter would move forward; if it were moved forward, the helicopter would move to the left, and so on, 90 degrees out of phase. Whether the pitch horns are ahead or behind, the blade will depend on the mechanical linkage arrangement between the cyclic stick, swashplate, and pitch horns.

If pitch horns are 90 degrees ahead of the blade, pitch decrease of the blades take place as the horns pass the direction the cyclic stick is displaced. Blade pitch increase takes place as the horns pass the direction opposite to the displacement of the stick. If the horns are 90 degrees behind the blades, pitch decrease will take place as the horns pass the direction opposite to the displacement of the cyclic. Blade pitch increase takes place as the horns pass the direction of displacement.

In either case, however, blade pitch decrease takes place 90 degrees ahead of cyclic stick position, and blade pitch increase takes place 90 degrees after passing the cyclic stick position. Thus, maximum downward *deflection* of the rotor blades occurs in the same direction as cyclic stick displacement, and maximum upward deflection occurs in the opposite direction.

In other words, when the cyclic stick is displaced forward, the swashplate's non-rotating disc tilts forward, and the swashplate's rotating disc follows this forward tilt. Since the mechanical linkage from the rotating disc to the rotor blades' pitch horns is 90 degrees ahead or behind the cyclic pitch change, the pitch angle is decreased as the rotor blades pass 90 degrees to the pilot's right and increased as the rotor blades pass 90 degrees to the pilot's left. Because of gyroscopic precession, maximum blade deflection occurs 90 degrees later in the cycle of motion. Thus, maximum downward deflection is forward; in the same direction as cyclic stick placement; and maximum upward deflection is aft, causing the rotor disc to tilt forward in the same direction as cyclic stick placement.

Main Rotor System

Fully articulated rotor systems (Fig. 5-3) generally consist of three or more rotor blades. In a fully articulated rotor system, each rotor blade is attached to the rotor hub by a horizontal hinge, called the *flapping hinge*, which permits the blades to flap up or down. Each blade can move up or down independently of the others. The flapping hinge can be located at varying distances from the rotor hub, and there can be more than one. The position is chosen by each manufacturer, primarily with regard to stability and control.

Each rotor blade is also attached to the hub by a vertical hinge, called a *drag* or *lag hinge*, which permits each blade, independently of the others, to move back and forth in the plane of the rotor disc. This forward and backward movement is called *dragging, lead-drag,* or *hunting*. The location of this hinge is chosen with primary regard to controlling vibration. Dampers are normally associated with the fully articulated system to prevent excessive motion about the drag hinge (Fig. 5-4).

Also, the blades can be *feathered* or rotated about their spanwise axis. Feathering means the automatic and periodic changing of the pitch angle of the rotor blades.

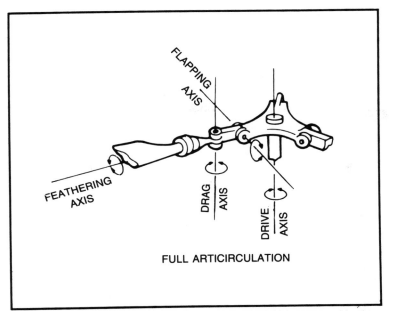

FULL ARTICIRCULATION

Fig. 5-3. A rotor system employing hinges about the flapping, drag, and feathering axes is said to be "fully articulated."

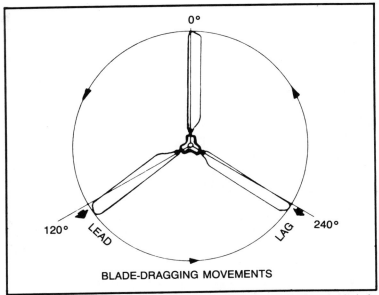

BLADE-DRAGGING MOVEMENTS

Fig. 5-4. Lead-lag action occurs around the drag-hinge axis of each blade in flight, as shown here, due to Coriolis effect.

A semirigid rotor system's rotor blades are rigidly interconnected to the hub, but the hub is free to tilt and rock with respect to the rotor shaft. In this system, only two-bladed rotors are used. The rotor flaps as a unit; that is, as one blade flaps up, the other blade automatically flaps down an equal amount.

The hinge which permits the flapping or seesaw effect is called a *teetering hinge*. The rocking hinge that allows this teetering mo-

Fig. 5-5. The MBB (Bölkow) 105 is one of few production helicopters to employ a rigid rotor. There are no flapping hinges; instead, the limberness of the rotor blades allows flapping action to occur.

tion is perpendicular to the teetering hinge and parallel to the rotor blades. This hinge allows the head to rock in response to the tilting of the swashplate by the cyclic pitch control, thus changing the pitch angle an equal amount on each blade, decreasing it on one and increasing it on the other.

The rotor blades of a semirigid rotor system may or may not require drag hinges, depending on whether the system is *underslung*. In an underslung system, the rotor blades lie in a plane below the plane containing the rotor hub pivot point. Because of coning, normal rotor operating rpm will place the center of mass of the rotor blades in approximately the same plane as the rotor hub pivot point. Consequently,the distance of the center of mass from the axis of rotation varies very little. Therefore, an underslung system is subject to Coriolis effect, but to a lesser degree than a system that's not underslung. Drag hinges aren't needed, since the hunting action can be absorbed through blade bending.

Collective pitch control changes the pitch of each blade simultaneously and an equal amount, either increasing the pitch of both or decreasing the pitch of both.

In rigid rotor system, the blades and mast are rigid with respect to each other. The blades can't flap or drag, but they can be feathered.

Because of their inflexibility, the rigid rotor system isn't one of the most popular. It's only been in the past few years that a great deal of progress has been made with its applications. One popular production helicopter that does employ this system is the MBB (Bölkow) 105 (Fig. 5-5).

6

Flight Maneuvers: The Takeoff

It should be obvious that the variable factors of wind, temperature, humidity, and gross weight greatly affect helicopter operation. Even when flying the same model, two flights are seldom exactly alike.

It would be impossible for a handbook such as this one to outline a specific nose attitude or power setting for a given flight regime (these will be discussed in another chapter). The following maneuvers are accomplished in what can only be described as normal day conditions with the helicopter responding normally.

Although helicopter controls were discussed in an earlier chapter, a summary of their effects from the pilot's point of view will be helpful in understanding the various flying maneuvers presented in following chapters.

The cyclic or cyclic pitch control tilts the rotor disc in the same direction as the cyclic is moved, and the helicopter moves in that direction. Thus, a backward displacement of the cyclic results in a nose-up tendency, followed by rearward flight; a sideward displacement results in a sideways tilt and sideways flight, etc. In normal, cruise flight, the cyclic is used much as is the yoke or joystick in a fixed-wing airplane. The main difference is that if a rearward displacement were held for long, the craft would, after climbing and losing airspeed, tend to fly backwards.

The collective, or collective pitch control, in hovering flight is used to stabilize the helicopter's vertical movement. Raise the collective and the helicopter climbs; lower it and the craft descends.

The primary effect of the collective is to control the engine's power (manifold pressure). If constant rotor rpm is maintained, the power will vary with the collective's position. Varying rpm is another collective function.

The twist-grip throttle control on the end of the collective is primarily used to control engine rpm. As stated above, the collective, to a certain degree, controls engine rpm, but the throttle is a considerable aid in maintaining rpm. It's often used by the pilot as a fine adjustment and can be used to obtain any desired rpm over the normal engine rpm range. Its second function is an alteration in power, and a small change can often result in a considerable change in boost.

The antitorque (rudder) pedals are used in powered flight to balance torque and to turn the craft in the yawing plane. As in an airplane, application of left rudder tends to yaw or turn the nose of the helicopter to the left and vice versa. In gliding flight (autorotation), rudder control is still available to maintain balanced flight or to turn.

The initial complexity of control coordination will be appreciated when it is stated that as one control is moved the other controls must generally be moved as well, especially in hovering maneuvers. As an example, consider the case of a helicopter about to move forward from a hover.

The stick is eased forward. The aircraft starts to move forward, but because of the loss of the ground bubble, it also begins to sink. As up collective is applied to maintain the desired height, the throttle position must be altered to maintain rpm, which in turn changes torque. This means that the rudder pedal position must also be altered to maintain the desired heading. The change in rudder position affects the sideways drifting tendency, rpm and so on. When any forward speed builds up, the rotor disc will tend to flap backwards and more forward cyclic must be applied.

However, the control that consistently causes the most difficulty is the throttle. It's this twist-grip power control that has a direct or indirect action-reaction on all other controls. Increase or decrease power, and rudder, cyclic, and collective adjustments must be made also.

Vertical Takeoff to a Hover

A vertical takeoff is a maneuver in which the helicopter is raised vertically from a spot on the ground to the normal hovering altitude, with a minimum of lateral and/or fore and aft movement.

To begin with, have the chopper headed into the wind. This is done to lessen complications when simplicity is the student's main need. As your proficiency rises, this maneuver will be less of a problem. Place the cyclic in a neutral position, and make sure the collective is in the full down position.

Make sure the craft is running in a warmed-up condition. You should now be sitting comfortably, with your feet on the pedals, right hand on the cyclic and left hand gripping the throttle control of the collective.

Open the throttle smoothly to acquire and maintain proper operating rpm. Raise the collective in a smooth, continuous movement, coordinating the throttle to maintain proper rpm. As the collective is increased and the craft becomes light on its skids (wheels or floats), torque will tend to cause the nose to swing to the right, unless you add a sufficient amount of left pedal pressure to maintain a constant heading.

As the helicopter becomes light on its skids, make the necessary control adjustments: cyclic corrections to ensure a level attitude on becoming airborne; pedal corrections to maintain heading; and collective corrections to ensure continuous vertical ascent to the desired hovering altitude.

When the desired hovering altitude has been reached, adjust throttle and collective as required to maintain rpm and altitude. Coordinate pedal changes with throttle and collective adjustments to maintain heading. Use the cyclic as necessary to maintain a constant position over the spot. Remember, the collective controls altitude, while the cyclic controls attitude and position.

Now, in a relatively stable position, check things out: engine and control operation, manifold pressure to hold hover, and cyclic stick position. Cyclic position will vary with the amount and distribution of load and wind speed (Fig. 6-1).

Errors

☐ **Failure to maintain level attitude upon becoming airborne**. Any number of items can cause this, but to a greater degree it's caused by not anticipating the actions and reactions of elements present. Not to worry; this will come with practice.

☐ **Pulling through on the collective after becoming airborne, causing the helicopter to gain too much altitude too quickly**. This, in turn, will necessitate a

Fig. 6-1. In a downwind or aft-CG liftoff to a hover, the tail will ride slightly low. Shown here is a Brantly 305, one of few five-place piston helicopters on the market.

comparatively large throttle and collective change, which will, in turn, produce even a greater degree of a problem, if not anticipated.

☐ **Overcontrolling the antitorque pedals,** which not only changes the heading of the helicopter but also changes rpm, necessitating a constant throttle adjustment.

☐ **Reducing throttle too rapidly in situations where proper rpm has been exceeded,** which usually means violent changes of heading to the left and dramatic loss of lift, resulting in loss of altitude.

Normal Takeoff from Hover

Takeoff from a hover is an orderly transition to forward flight and is executed to increase altitude safely and expeditiously.

After lifting the helicopter to a normal hover, check the engine and control operations. Note the cyclic stick position to determine if the copter is loaded properly. Check the manifold pressure required to hover to determine the amount of excess power available.

Make a 360 degree spot turn for clearing the area all around. Slowly, yet smoothly, ease the cyclic forward. Apply just enough forward cyclic to start the craft moving forward over the ground.

As the machine starts to move forward, increase collective as necessary to prevent settling when it departs ground effect. Adjust throttle to maintain rpm lost because of collective increase. The increase in power will, in turn, require an increase in left pedal to stay on heading. Keep a straight takeoff path throughout the maneuver, if necessary, picking two reference points.

As you accelerate to effective translational lift and the helicopter beings to climb, the nose will begin to pitch up due to increased lift. Compensate for this nose-up tendency by adjusting collective to normal climb power, and apply enough forward cyclic to overcome nose pitching. Hold an altitude that will allow a smooth acceleration toward climbing airspeed and a commensurate gain in altitude so that the takeoff profile will not take you through any of the cross-hatched area or the height/velocity chart for that particular helicopter (see helicopter flight manual chapter). As airspeed increases, the streamlining of a fuselage will reduce engine torque effect, requiring a gradual reduction of left pedal pressure.

As the chopper continues to climb and airspeed approaches normal climb speed, apply rear cyclic pressure to raise the nose smoothly to the normal climb attitude. The normal climb attitude is approximately the attitude of the machine when it's sitting on level ground (Fig. 6-2).

Errors

☐ **Failure to use sufficient collective to prevent settling between the time the helicopter leaves ground effect to when it picks up translational lift.**

☐ **Adding power too rapidly at the beginning of the transition from hovering to forward flight without forward cyclic compensation,** thus causing the craft to gain excessive altitude before acquiring airspeed.

☐ **Assuming an extreme nose-down attitude near the ground in the transition from hovering to forward flight.**

☐ **Failure to maintain a straight flight track over the ground.**

☐ **Failure to keep proper airspeed during the climb.**

☐ **Failure to adjust the throttle to maintain proper rpm.**

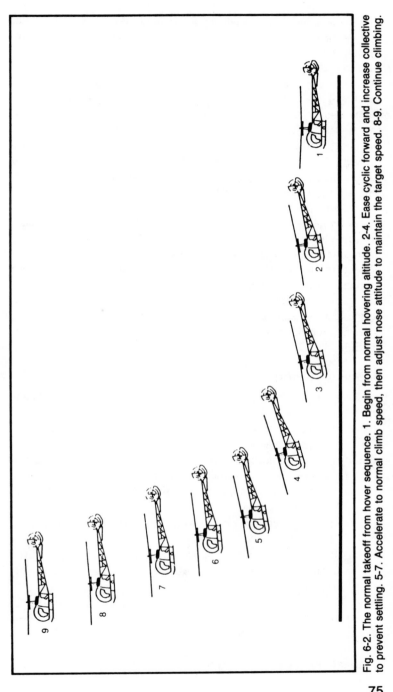

Fig. 6-2. The normal takeoff from hover sequence. 1. Begin from normal hovering altitude. 2-4. Ease cyclic forward and increase collective to prevent settling. 5-7. Accelerate to normal climb speed, then adjust nose attitude to maintain the target speed. 8-9. Continue climbing.

Note: If, for some reason, a takeoff can't be made into the wind, and a crosswind takeoff must be made, fly the helicopter in a slip during the early stages of the maneuver. To do this, the cyclic is held into the wind to maintain the selected ground track for takeoff, while the heading is kept straight along the takeoff path with rudder. Thus, the ground track and the fuselage are aligned with each other. In other words, the rotor is tilted into the wind to allow the aircraft to slip into the wind as much as the wind is pushing the copter sideways, effectively cancelling the wind's effect. To prevent the nose from turning in the direction of rotor tilt, you'll have to increase pedal pressure on the side opposite the rotor tilt. The stronger the crosswind, the greater the amount of rotor tilt and rudder pressure.

After gaining approximately 50 feet of altitude, establish a heading into the wind (crab), by coordinating a turn into the wind to maintain the desired ground track. The stronger the crosswind component, the more the chopper will have to be turned into the wind to maintain desired ground track. Once straight-and-level flight on the desired heading is reached, continue to use the rudders as necessary to compensate for torque to keep the craft in trim. Otherwise, there will be no other rudder correction for the wind in the crab attitude.

Running Takeoff

The *running takeoff* is used when conditions of load and/or density altitude prevent a sustained hover at normal hovering altitude. It's often referred to as a *high-altitude takeoff*. With insufficient power to hover, at least momentarily or at a very low altitude, a running takeoff is not advisable. No takeoff should be attempted if the helicopter can't be lifted off the ground momentarily at full power. There are two main reasons why this is always so:

☐ If the helicopter can't hover, its performance is unpredictable.
☐ If the helicopter can't be raised off the ground at all, sufficient power might not be available for a safe running takeoff.

A safe running takeoff can be accomplished only if ground area of sufficient length and smoothness is available and if no barriers exist in the flight path to interfere with a shallow climb.

Head the copter directly into the wind. Increase throttle to ob-

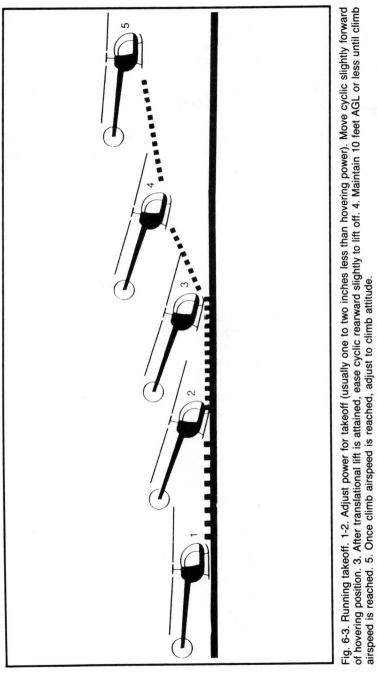

Fig. 6-3. Running takeoff. 1-2. Adjust power for takeoff (usually one to two inches less than hovering power). Move cyclic slightly forward of hovering position. 3. After translational lift is attained, ease cyclic rearward slightly to lift off. 4. Maintain 10 feet AGL or less until climb airspeed is reached. 5. Once climb airspeed is reached, adjust to climb attitude.

tain takeoff rpm. Hold cyclic slightly forward of the hovering "neutral" position. Raise collective slowly to one or two inches below that required to hover or until the craft starts to accelerate forward.

Maintain a straight ground track with both lateral cyclic and rudders for heading until a climb is established. As effective translational lift is attained, slight back pressure on the cyclic will take the helicopter into flight smoothly, in a level attitude, with little or no pitching (Fig. 6-3).

Don't exceed 10 feet AGL, to allow airspeed to build to normal climb speed. Follow a climb profile that will take you through the clear area of the height/velocity curve for your particular helicopter.

During practice maneuvers, climb to 50 feet AGL, and then adjust power to normal climb and attitude to normal climb.

Errors

☐ **Failure to align heading and ground track to keep ground friction to a minimum.**

☐ **Attempting to pull the helicopter off the ground before translational lift is obtained.**

☐ **Lowering the nose too much after becoming airborne, resulting in the helicopter settling back to the ground.**

☐ **Failure to remain below approximately 10 feet AGL until airspeed approaches normal climb speed.**

Maximum Performance Takeoff

A *maximum performance takeoff* is used to climb at a steep angle in order to clear barriers in the flight path. It can be used when taking off from small fields that are surrounded by high obstacles. Before attempting such a maneuver, though, thoroughly understand the capabilities and limitations of your equipment and the environment in which you're flying. Take into consideration the wind velocity, density altitude, gross weight of your machine and its CG location, as well as other factors affecting your technique and the performance characteristics of your craft.

To safely make such a takeoff more than sufficient power to hover must be available to prevent the chopper from sinking back to the ground after becoming airborne. This maneuver will result

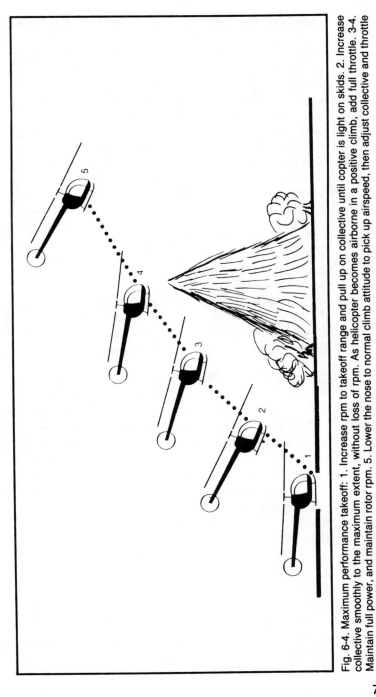

Fig. 6-4. Maximum performance takeoff: 1. Increase rpm to takeoff range and pull up on collective until copter is light on skids. 2. Increase collective smoothly to the maximum extent, without loss of rpm. 3-4. Maintain full power, and maintain rotor rpm. 5. Lower the nose to normal climb attitude to pick up airspeed, then adjust collective and throttle to continue a normal climbout.

in a steep climb, affording maximum altitude gain over a minimum distance forward.

The angle of climb for this type takeoff depends on existing conditions. The more critical these conditions—high density altitude, calm wind, etc.—the shallower the angle of climb. Use extreme caution in making a steep climb. If the airspeed is allowed to get too low, the craft could settle back to the ground.

Consult the height/velocity chart for your particular helicopter. An engine failure at low altitude and airspeed would place the helicopter in a dangerous position, requiring a high degree of skill in making a safe autorotative landing. It could be necessary to operate in the shaded area of the height/velocity chart during the beginning of this maneuver when operating in a light or no-wind condition.

The angle of climb and resulting airspeed will be dictated by the proximity and height of obstacles to be cleared. You must be aware of the calculated risk involved when operating in the shaded area of the height/velocity chart.

The first step in a maximum performance takeoff should be to head into the wind, with the cyclic placed in what would normally be the neutral position for hovering. Check this position by hovering the helicopter momentarily prior to preparing to execute the maneuver.

Establish the proper rpm setting and apply sufficient collective to lighten the craft on its skids. Apply the maximum amount of collective that can be obtained without reducing rpm. Simultaneously add full throttle, and apply sufficient forward cyclic to establish a forward climbing attitude as the craft leaves the ground.

Use rudder pedals as necessary to maintain heading. Do not sacrifice rpm in order to obtain increased pitch on the rotor blades. If rpm starts to decrease under a full power condition, it can be regained *only by reducing collective.*

Use full power until the helicopter is clear of all obstacles, then a normal climb may be established and the power reduced (Fig. 6-4).

Errors

- ☐ **Too much forward initially,** allowing the nose to go down too far.
- ☐ **Failure to maintain maximum permissible rpm.**
- ☐ **Movement of controls too abrupt.**

7

Flight Maneuvers: The Hover

To a ground observer or even a passenger, hovering may look simple, because the pilot is apparently doing little and the helicopter is virtually motionless above the ground. However, since you've tried your hand at this maneuver—or are about to—you should know that this isn't completely true: The pilot is maintaining position with the cyclic, keeping a fixed height with the collective, retaining the desired heading with rudder pedals, and correcting any changes or rpm with the throttle.

The maneuver requires a high degree of concentration on your part as the pilot. Control corrections should be pressure rather than abrupt movements: A constant pressure on the desired rudder pedal will result in a smooth turn, while pronounced movements will tend to jerk the nose around, causing other complications.

Smoothness on the controls can be accomplished by immediately making all corrections and not waiting out helicopter movement. Stopping and stabilizing the machine at a hover requires a number of small, pressure corrections to avoid overcontrolling. With practice, it becomes easier to anticipate the helicopter's movements.

The attitude of the copter determines its movements over the ground. While the attitude required to hover varies with the wind conditions and center of gravity (CG) locations, there's a particular attitude which can be found by experimentation that will keep the craft hovering over a selected point. After this attitude has been discovered, deviations can be easily noted and the necessary corrections made, often before the helicopter actually starts to move. This is really flying by the seat of your pants.

Coordination of all controls can't be overemphasized. Any change on one control will almost always require a correction on one or more of the other controls. Hovering can be accomplished in a precise manner by keeping in mind the small, smooth and coordinated control responses (Figs. 7-1, 7-2).

Errors

- [ ] **Tenseness**, which often causes late reactions to helicopter movements, or overreaction resulting in overcorrecting.
- [ ] **Failure to allow for lag in cyclic and collective**, which also leads to overcontrolling.
- [ ] **Confusing altitude changes for attitude changes**, resulting in the use of improper cockpit controls.
- [ ] **Hovering too high, out of ground effect.**
- [ ] **Hovering too low**, resulting in occasional touchdown.

Hovering Turn

The hovering turn is a maneuver performed at hovering alti-

Fig. 7-1. Hovering in ground effect requires less power than hovering 100 feet in the air.

Fig. 7-2. An Enstrom F-28A hovers in ground effect during agricultural spray operations.

tude. The nose of the helicopter is rotated either left or right, while maintaining position over a reference point on the ground. It requires the coordination of all flight controls and demands precision movement near the ground.

In calm air a hovering turn is simple, but in a wind condition, the helicopter will be alternately moving forward, sideward, backward, sideward and then forward again, while turning on its axis. Also, the weather-vaning stability of the copter is such that the initial turn out of the wind will be resisted, and on passing the downwind position the rate of turn will tend to speed up. Again, due to the wind, a fair amount of rudder will be necessary to make and control the turn, and this will have a considerable effect on the rpm.

Keeping the above factors in mind, the turn is accomplished with a feel for the helicopter's movements and by staying on top of the situation.

Start the maneuver from a normal hovering altitude, headed into the wind. Begin by applying rudder pressure smoothly in the direction you desire to turn.

When the nose begins to turn, and throughout the remainder of the turn, use cyclic to maintain position over the ground reference point. Use rudder pedals to maintain slow, constant rate of turn. Collective, along with the throttle, is used to maintain a constant altitude and rpm.

As the 180-degree position is approached in the turn, anticipate the use of a small amount of opposite rudder, as the tail of the helicopter swings from a position into the wind to one downwind. The machine will have a tendency to whip or increase its rate of turn as a result of the weather-vaning tendency of the tail. Remember, the higher the wind, the greater will be this whipping action.

As you approach the desired heading for turn completion, apply opposite pedal pressure as necessary to stop the turn on this heading.

During the hovering turn to the left, the rpm will decrease if power isn't reduced slightly. This is due to the amount of engine power that's being absorbed by the tail rotor, which is dependent upon the pitch angle at which the tail rotor blades are operating. Avoid making large corrections in rpm while turning, since the throttle adjustment will result in erratic nose movements due to torque changes.

Always make the first hovering turn to the left to determine the amount of left pedal available. If a 90-degree turn to the left can't be made, or if an unusual amount of pedal is required to complete a 45-degree hovering turn to the left, don't attempt a turn to the right, since sufficient left pedal might not be available to prevent an uncontrolled turn. Hover power requires a large amount of left pedal to maintain heading. Once the turn has started, sufficient left pedal in excess of this amount must be available to prevent an uncontrolled turn to the right.

Hovering turns should be avoided in winds strong enough to preclude sufficient back cyclic control to maintain the helicopter on the selected ground reference point when headed downwind. Check the craft's flight manual for the manufacturer's recommendations on this limit.

Errors

- ☐ **Failure to maintain a slow, constant rate of turn.**
- ☐ **Failure to maintain position over the reference point.**
- ☐ **Failure to keep the rpm within normal operating ranges.**
- ☐ **Failure to make the first turn to the left.**

□ **Failure to maintain a constant altitude.**
□ **Failure to apply rudder smoothly and cautiously.**

Hovering Forward Flight

This maneuver is not so much a hover as it is keeping the helicopter from getting away from you, in what could be labelled as slow flight near the ground. Forward, hovering flight can generally be used to move the chopper to a specific area, unless strong winds prohibit crosswind or downwind hovering. A hovering turn is utilized to head the helicopter in the direction of the desired area, then forward flight at a slow speed is used to move to that area. During this maneuver, a constant, slow ground speed, altitude, and heading should be maintained. Care should be taken so as not to leave the ground-cushion effect (Figs. 7-3, 7-4).

Pick two reference points in front of and in line with the helicopter. These points can be any object that can be clearly seen. Keep them in line throughout the maneuver, since they guarantee a straight ground track while you're on the move.

Initiate the maneuver from a normal, hovering altitude by applying slight forward pressure on the cyclic—only enough at first to start the helicopter moving.

As the craft begins to move, return the cyclic toward the neutral position to keep the ground speed at a slow rate—no faster than normal walking pace. Ground effect will be retained at this speed, thus reducing the need for power and pedal corrections.

Keep a constant check on your reference points. Control ground speed with the cyclic, a steady heading with the pedals, a constant altitude with the collective and proper operating rpm with the throttle.

Upon reaching your desired area, apply gradual, rearward cyclic until the helicopter's forward movement stops. The cyclic must be returned to the neutral position when movement stops or rearward flight will begin. Forward movement can also be stopped by simply applying enough rearwind cyclic to level the helicopter and let it coast or drift to a stop. However, the rearward cyclic pressure will require more lead time in this instance.

Errors

□ **Erratic movement of the cyclic**, resulting in overcontrolling and an uneven movement over the ground.

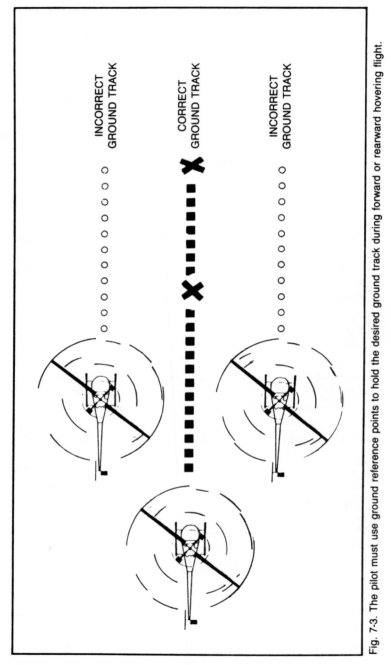

INCORRECT GROUND TRACK

CORRECT GROUND TRACK

INCORRECT GROUND TRACK

Fig. 7-3. The pilot must use ground reference points to hold the desired ground track during forward or rearward hovering flight.

Fig. 7-4. While the pilot may be tempted to look out at the horizon during hover, true position information cannot be gained that way; instead, the pilot should focus at a reference point 10 to 20 feet forward, on the ground. Here, a Brantly B-2B is shown hovering.

- ☐ **Failure to use proper rudder procedures**, resulting in excessive nose movement.
- ☐ **Failure to maintain a hovering altitude.**
- ☐ **Failure to maintain proper rpm.**

Hover to Hover

This is a form of a longer-distance air taxi and is frequently used as a coordination exercise. It shouldn't be confused with a "quick-stop" (discussed later), which is an advanced exercise carried out more quickly and one in which the rotor is autorotating at one stage during the maneuver.

The transition to another area consists of a hover, then a gradual acceleration forward into the wind to about 60 mph, then a gradual return to a hover again. It's accomplished at a fixed altitude of about 20 feet AGL—higher than that of a normal hover.

The first part of the transition isn't too difficult. The technique is much like beginning a forward climb. Initiate forward pressure on the cyclic to get forward movement; slight up collective when ground resonance is lost, to hold altitude; rudder position to maintain heading; and an increase in throttle to regain rpm lost when collective was raised. You should now be in straight and level flight.

It's the slowing down upon reaching your objective that calls for careful attention. Ease back on the cyclic—this should be a very small movement—accompanied, or even preceded, by a downward movement on the collective. A corresponding change of a rudder pedal position is needed to maintain heading and a change of throttle to retain correct rpm.

When slowing down, translational lift will be lost. Power must again be increased, with a corresponding balancing of torque and rpm.

Errors

☐ **Failure to maintain altitude when entering translational lift.**
☐ **Losing or gaining rpm.**
☐ **Uncoordination on controls.**
☐ **Failure to maintain altitude when leaving translational lift.**
☐ **Moving too fast or slow between the two areas.**

Hovering Sideward Flight

It could become necessary to move a helicopter to a specific area or position when conditions make it impossible to use forward flight. In such a case, sideward flight may be a possible solution. It's also an excellent coordination maneuver. The primary objective is to maintain a constant ground speed, altitude and heading (Fig. 7-5).

Begin the maneuver by picking two reference points in a line running in the direction sideward flight is to be made. These two points will help you maintain proper ground tracking. Keep these reference points in line throughout the maneuver.

Initiate hovering sideward flight from a normal hovering altitude by applying sideward pressure on the cyclic in the direction you want to move.

As movement begins, return the cyclic toward the neutral position, but not all the way to neutral. Adjust to keep a slow ground speed. Remember, ground effect will be retained, thus reducing the need for power or rudder corrections, at the speed of a walking person.

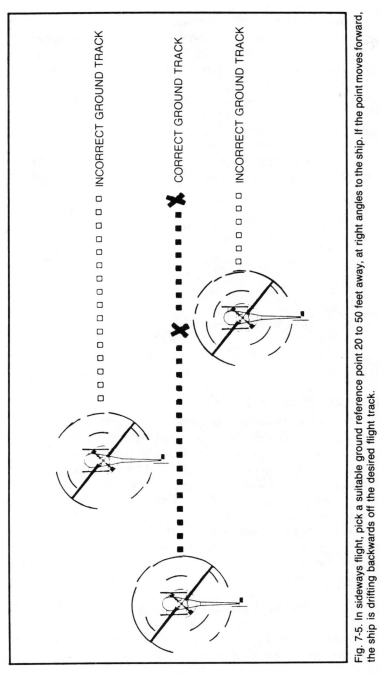

Fig. 7-5. In sideways flight, pick a suitable ground reference point 20 to 50 feet away, at right angles to the ship. If the point moves forward, the ship is drifting backwards off the desired flight track.

During the complete maneuver, maintain a constant ground speed and ground track with the cyclic; a constant heading perpendicular to the proposed ground track with the rudder, a constant altitude with the collective; and proper operating rpm with the throttle.

Apply cyclic pressure in the opposite direction to that of the helicopter's movement and hold until the craft comes almost to a stop. As the motion ceases, the cyclic must be returned to the neutral position to prevent movement in the other direction. Sideward movement also can be stopped by simply applying enough opposite cyclic pressure to only level the helicopter. It will then drift to a stop.

Errors

- [ ] **Movement of the cyclic is erratic**, resulting in over-control and uneven movement over the ground.
- [ ] **Failure to use proper rudder control**, resulting in excessive nose movement.
- [ ] **Failure to maintain a hovering altitude.**
- [ ] **Failure to maintain proper rpm.**
- [ ] **Failure to make clearing turns prior to starting the maneuver.**

Hovering Rearward Flight

This maneuver may be necessary to move the helicopter to a specific area when forward or sideward flight can't be used, as in backing into a parking pad surrounded by other craft.

As with previous maneuvers, pick out two reference points in front of, and in line with, the helicopter. These will help you in keeping a proper ground track. Keep these reference points in line throughout the flight.

Start rearwind flight from a normal hovering altitude by applying rearward pressure on the stick. After movement has started, position the cyclic to maintain a slow enough ground speed that ground effect is maintained.

Keep a constant ground speed with the cyclic; a constant heading with the rudder; a constant altitude with the collective; and proper rpm with the throttle.

To stop rearward movement, apply forward cyclic and hold until the helicopter almost stops. As the motion does stop, return the cyclic to the neutral position. Also, as was the case with forward and sideward flight, forward cyclic can be used to level the helicopter, letting it drift to a stop.

Errors

☐ **Overcontrolling and the uneven movement over the ground**, due to erratic movement of the cyclic.
☐ **Excessive nose movements**, due to improper use of rudder.
☐ **Failure to maintain hovering altitude.**
☐ **Failure to maintain proper operating rpm.**
☐ **Failure to make clearing turns before starting.**

8
Flight Maneuvers

Flight in which a constant altitude and heading are maintained is considered *Straight and level*. The straight and level flight attitude is the pitch attitude of the helicopter necessary to maintain straight and level flight. The level-flight attitude is the attitude of the helicopter necessary to maintain altitude. In aeronautical argot, straight and level flight, turns, climbs, and descents are often called *air work*.

Straight-and-Level

Airspeed is determined by the attitude of the helicopter. The attitude of the copter is controlled by the cyclic. Altitude is maintained by the use of the collective and throttle. In order to maintain forward flight, the rotor tip path plane must be tilted forward to obtain the necessary horizontal thrust component from the main rotor. This will generally result in a nose-low attitude. The lower the nose, the greater the power required to maintain altitude and the higher the resulting airspeed. Conversely, the greater the power used, the lower the nose must be to maintain altitude (Figs. 8-1, 8-2).

When in straight and level flight, an increase in collective while holding airspeed constant with the cyclic causes the craft to climb; a decrease in collective while holding airspeed constant causes a descent. A correction on the collective requires a coordinated correction on the throttle in order to maintain a constant rpm, plus

Fig. 8-1. In cruise flight, the helicopter will ride nose-low. Since there are no airframe references, the pilot must monitor altitude excursions on the altimeter. Attempting to hold a constant airspeed will usually preclude wild altitude changes.

Fig. 8-2. A Hughes 500D in cruise over Southern California. The 500D, at 150 knots, cruises faster than many small airplanes.

a correction on the rudder pedals to maintain heading and longitudinal trim. Always strive to maintain coordinated flight without either slipping or skidding the helicopter.

To increase airspeed in straight and level flight, increase collective for more power, then gently apply forward pressure on the cyclic to maintain altitude. To decrease airspeed, decrease collective for reduced power, then add back pressure on the cyclic to maintain altitude.

As previously stated, you should expect a slight delay in control reaction from the time of correction input and the machine's response. The cyclic stick seems to be more prone to this delay than other controls. In making cyclic corrections to control the attitude or airspeed, take care not to overcontrol. Try to anticipate actual helicopter movement. If the nose of the craft rises above the level flight attitude, apply forward cyclic pressure to bring it down. If this correction is held too long, the nose will drop too low. Put in your correction, then wait for the resulting reaction. This is especially important, since the helicopter will continue to change attitude momentarily after you replace the controls to neutral, so anticipate such action by bringing controls back to the neutral position just prior to reaching the desired attitude.

Most helicopters are inherently unstable. If gusts or turbulence cause the nose to drop, it will tend to continue dropping, instead of returning to a straight and level attitude. You must remain alert and fly the helicopter at all times.

Errors

- [ ] **Failure to trim properly.**
- [ ] **Tending to hold pedal pressure and opposite cyclic** (cross controlling).
- [ ] **Failure to hold best airspeed.** Aft cyclic pressure dissipated airspeed without significant climb.
- [ ] **Failure to recognize proper control position for maintaining crab-type drift corrections.**

Turns

This basic maneuver is used to change the heading of your craft. The aerodynamics of the turn have been discussed in previous chapters—lift components, vertical lift, resultant lift, load factors, etc. They should be thoroughly understood.

Before beginning, clear the area above, below, and all around. This should be standard procedure with any maneuver. Enter the turn from straight and level flight. Apply sideward pressure on the cyclic in the direction of desired flight. This should be the only control movement necessary to start the turn.

Note: Don't use the antitorque pedals to assist the turn. Use the pedals only to compensate for torque in keeping the helicopter in trim longitudinally.

The more the cyclic is displaced, the steeper the resulting angle of bank. Therefore, adjust the cyclic to obtain, and maintain, the desired bank angle throughout the maneuver. Increase collective as necessary to maintain altitude, at the same time coordinating throttle to keep desired rpm. Increase left pedal pressure to counteract the added torque effect from the increased power. Depending on the angle of bank, swiftness of entry, power changes, etc., additional forward or rearward cyclic pressure may be necessary: forward pressure to maintain airspeed, or rearward pressure to keep the nose from falling out of the turn.

Recovery from the turn is the same as the entry, except the pressure on the cyclic is applied in reverse. Since the helicopter will continue to turn as long as it's in a bank, start the rollout before reaching the desired heading. Rollout lead time is normally expressed in degrees, as you will usually be turning to headings. A rule-of-thumb is 5 to 10 degrees lead time for angle of banks up to 30 degrees, and 10 to 15 degrees lead time for more than 30.

Make climbing and descending turns the same as in straight and level, except that the helicopter will now be in a climbing or descending attitude. Establish entry by merely combining the techniques of both maneuvers—climb or descent entry and turn entry.

In a descending turn, however, an unusual feature occurs, especially noticeable to fixed-wing pilots. The craft can be turning to the left, but a considerable amount of right rudder is necessary to maintain balanced flight due to the low rotor torque.

A *skid* occurs when the helicopter slides sideways away from the center of the turn. It's caused by too much rudder pressure in the direction of the turn or too little in the direction opposite the turn in relation to the amount of collective (power) used. If the helicopter is forced to turn faster, with increased pedal pressure instead of increasing the degree of bank, it will skid sideways away from the center of the turn. Instead of flying in its normal, curved pattern, it will fly a straighter course. You could liken it to an automobile skid. If the steering wheel is the rudder, it's applying too much steering wheel for the speed or for the sharpness of the turn. Like the automobile, the helicopter will skid sideways in regards to the direction of wanted travel.

In a right climbing turn, if insufficient left pedal is applied to compensate for increased torque effect, a skid will occur. In a left climbing turn, if excessive left pedal is applied to compensate for increased torque effect, a skid will occur.

In a right descending turn, if excessive right pedal is applied to compensate for decreased torque, a skid will occur. In a left descending turn, if insufficient right pedal is applied to compensate for the decreased torque effect, a skid will occur.

A skid can also occur when flying straight and level, if the nose of the helicopter is allowed to move sideways along the horizon. This condition occurs when improper pedal pressure is held to counteract torque, and the copter is held level with cyclic control.

A *slip* occurs when the helicopter slides sideways toward the center of the turn. It's caused by an insufficient amount of pedal in the direction of turn or too much in the direction opposite the turn, in relationship to the amount of collective or power used. In other words, if improper pedal pressure is held, keeping the nose from following the turn, the craft will slip sideways into (toward the center of) the turn.

In a right climbing turn, if excessive left pedal is applied to compensate for the increased torque effect, a slip occurs. In a left climbing turn, if insufficient left pedal is applied to compensate for the increased torque effect, a slip also occurs.

In a right descending turn, if insufficient right pedal is applied to compensate for the decreased torque effect, a slip will occur. In a left descending turn, if excessive right pedal is applied to compensate for the decreased torque effect, a slip also occurs.

A slip can also occur in straight and level flight if one side of the helicopter is low and the nose is held straight by rudder pressure. This technique is used to correct for a crosswind during an approach and during a takeoff when at a low altitude.

Errors

- ☐ **Failure to hold altitude when entering, during, and exiting a turn.**
- ☐ **Using unnecessary pedal pressure for turns.** Pedal pressure isn't necessary for small helicopters.

Normal Climb

Since entry into a climb from a hover has already been discussed, this section will be limited to climb entry from normal cruising flight.

Begin the maneuver by first applying rearward cyclic pressure to obtain an approximate climb attitude. Simultaneously, increase collective until climb manifold pressure is established. Adjust the throttle to obtain, and maintain, climb rpm. An increase in left rudder pressure also is necessary to compensate for the increase in torque. As you approach the desired climb airspeed, further adjustment of the cyclic is necessary to establish and hold this airspeed.

Throughout the maneuver, keep climb attitude and airspeed with cyclic, climb manifold pressure and rpm with collective and throttle. Longitudinal trim and heading are maintained with the rudder pedals.

To level off from a climb, start adjusting to level flight attitude a few feet prior to reaching the desired altitude. The amount of lead you choose will depend on the rate of climb at the time of leveling off. The higher the rate of climb, the more the lead. Apply forward cyclic to adjust and keep a level flight attitude which will be slightly nose low. Maintain climb power until airspeed approaches cruise airspeed, then lower the collective to obtain cruising manifold pressure. Make a throttle adjustment to cruising rpm, and you're there. Throughout the level-off, maintain longitudinal trim and a constant heading with the rudders.

Errors

- ☐ **Failure to hold proper manifold pressure.**
- ☐ **Failure to hold proper airspeed.**
- ☐ **Holding too much or too little left rudder.**
- ☐ **In level-off, decreasing power before lowering the nose to cruising attitude.**

Normal Descent

To establish a normal descent from straight and level flight at cruising airspeed, lower collective to obtain proper manifold pressure, adjust throttle to maintain rpm, and increase right rudder pressure to maintain desired heading. If cruising airspeed is the same as, or slightly above descent airspeed, simultaneously apply the necessary cyclic stick pressure to obtain the approximate descending attitude. If cruising airspeed is well above descent airspeed, the level flight attitude may be maintained until the airspeed approaches descent airspeed, at which time the nose should be lowered to the descending attitude.

Throughout the maneuver, maintain descending attitude and airspeed with the cyclic control, descending manifold pressure and rpm with collective and throttle. Control heading with the rudders.

To level off from the descent, lead the desired altitude by an amount that will depend on the rate of descent at the time of level-off. Remember, the higher the rate of descent, the greater the lead. At this point, increase collective to obtain cruising manifold pressure, adjust throttle to maintain proper rpm, increase left rudder pressure to maintain heading, and adjust cyclic to obtain cruising airspeed and the level flight attitude as the desired altitude is reached.

Errors

☐ **Failure to hold constant angle of descent.**
☐ **Failure to adjust rudder pressures for power changes.**

9

Flight Maneuvers: Approach and Landing

An approach is a transition maneuver which is flown from traffic pattern altitude, at cruising speed, to a normal hover. It is basically a power glide, made at an angle of descent matching the type of approach desired (Fig. 9-1).

There are three basic approaches that you should be proficient in performing: *normal, steep* and *shallow*. You also should know how to analyze influential outside factors and how to plan an approach to fit any particular situation in which you find yourself.

Your choice of an approach is governed by the size of landing area, barriers in the approach path, type of ground surface, temperature, altitude, humidity (density altitude), wind direction, wind speed, and the gross weight of your craft. Give a little tolerance for overshooting or undershooting a chosen landing spot, and in order to maintain a maximum safety margin in each type of approach, retain translational lift as long as practicable.

Evaluation of existing wind conditions must be made before initiating an approach. Although the approach is generally made into the wind, conditions can indicate the entry will have to be made from a downwind or crosswind position. The traffic pattern is generally flown at normal cruise airspeed. The velocity of the wind determines the airspeed that will be maintained after the approach is started. Increase airspeed in proportion to any increase in wind velocity. Keep the angle of descent constant, regardless of wind speed.

Fig. 9-1. A Westland helicopter flares on the descent into LAX (Los Angeles International).

Crosswind approaches are made by crabbing or slipping or a combination of both. To make running landings in strong crosswinds, it may be necessary to touch down, initially, with the upwind skid (skid that's into the wind), to avoid drifting (Fig. 9-2).

Keep the rpm constant during all approaches. If rpm is allowed to fluctuate or change abruptly, variations or torque forces will cause the craft's fuselage to yaw around its vertical axis, and control will be difficult. To maintain proper directional control, make rpm changes and/or collective settings smoothly, accompanied by appropriate changes in pedal pressure.

Normal Approach to a Hover

Make a normal airport pattern entry at a 45-degree angle to the downwind leg in such a manner that the actual turn to the downwind leg will be accomplished opposite the middle one-third of the runway. The transition from the downwind leg to final approach can be made by two 90-degree turns in which a definite base leg is established or by a single 180-degree turn. Remember, at all times during this transition, keep sufficient altitude in case of engine failure. In such a case, you would want to make an autorotative land-

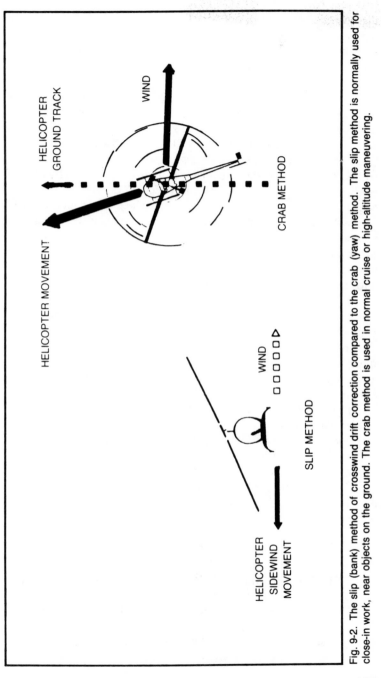

Fig. 9-2. The slip (bank) method of crosswind drift correction compared to the crab (yaw) method. The slip method is normally used for close-in work, near objects on the ground. The crab method is used in normal cruise or high-altitude maneuvering.

ing into the wind. This fact will determine the point in the traffic pattern where a power reduction is made.

Start the approach by lowering the collective the amount necessary to descend at approximately a 12 degree angle on the final approach leg. As the collective is lowered, increase right pedal as necessary to compensate for the change in torque to maintain heading. Adjust throttle to maintain proper rpm. Hold attitude with cyclic control until the airspeed nears approach speed, then adjust with the cyclic to the attitude that will maintain this approach speed.

The angle of descent and rate of descent are primarily controlled by collective; the airspeed is primarily controlled by the cyclic; and heading on final with the rudders. However, only with coordination of all controls can the approach be made successfully.

Maintain approach airspeed until the point on the circuit is reached where, through evaluation of apparent ground speed, it's determined that forward airspeed must be progressively decreased to arrive at hovering altitude and an attitude at the landing spot with a zero ground speed.

As forward airspeed is gradually reduced by applying rearward cyclic, additional power through the collective must be applied to compensate for the decrease in translational lift and to maintain the proper angle of descent. As collective is increased, left rudder must be increased to keep heading; throttle adjusted to hold rpm; and cyclic coordinated to maintain the proper change in forward airspeed.

The approach is terminated at hovering altitude above your intended landing point with zero ground speed. Very little, if any, additional power is required to stop the forward movement and rate of descent if power has been properly applied during the final portion of the approach.

If the condition of the landing spot is unknown, the approach may be terminated just short of the spot so it can be checked out before moving forward for touchdown (Fig. 9-3).

Errors

☐ **Failure to maintain proper rpm during the entire approach.**
☐ **Improper use of the collective in controlling the rate of descent.**
☐ **Failure to make rudder corrections to compensate for collective changes during the approach.**

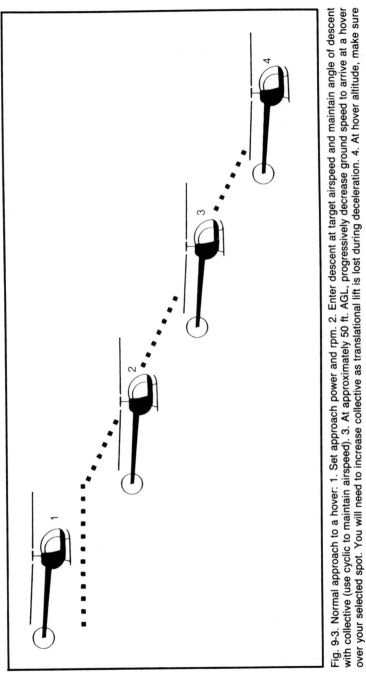

Fig. 9-3. Normal approach to a hover: 1. Set approach power and rpm. 2. Enter descent at target airspeed and maintain angle of descent with collective (use cyclic to maintain airspeed). 3. At approximately 50 ft. AGL, progressively decrease ground speed to arrive at a hover over your selected spot. You will need to increase collective as translational lift is lost during deceleration. 4. At hover altitude, make sure the craft is level.

☐ **Failure to arrive at hovering altitude, hovering attitude, and zero ground speed almost simultaneously.**

☐ **Low rpm in transition to the hover at the end of the approach.**

☐ **Using too much aft cyclic close to the ground,** which could result in the tail rotor striking the ground.

Note: During the early stages of a crosswind approach, a crab and/or slip may be used. During the final stages of the approach, beginning about 50 feet AGL, a slip should be used to align the fuselage with the ground track. The rotor is tilted into the wind with cyclic enough to cancel the wind drift. Heading is maintained along the ground track with the rudders. Use this technique on any type of crosswind approach—shallow, normal or steep.

Steep Approach to a Hover

A steep approach is used primarily when obstacles in the approach path are too high to allow a normal approach. It will permit entry into most confined areas. Use an approach angle of 12 to 20 degrees.

Entry is made in the same manner as a normal approach, except that a greater reduction of collective is required at the beginning of the approach to start the descent. As collective is lowered, increase right rudder pressure to maintain heading, and adjust throttle to hold rpm.

As in the normal approach, the angle and rate of descent are primarily controlled by collective pitch, and the airspeed is primarily controlled by the cyclic. However, only with the coordination of all controls can the approach be accomplished successfully.

Maintain approach airspeed until the point on the approach is reached where, through evaluation of apparent ground speed, it's determined that forward airspeed must be progressively decreased in order to arrive at hovering altitude at the intended landing spot with zero ground speed. This is very important, since a flare shouldn't be made near the ground due to the danger of the tail rotor striking.

As forward speed is gradually reduced by the application of rearward cyclic pressure, additional power from the collective must be applied to compensate for the decrease in translational lift and to maintain the proper angle of descent. As collective pitch is in-

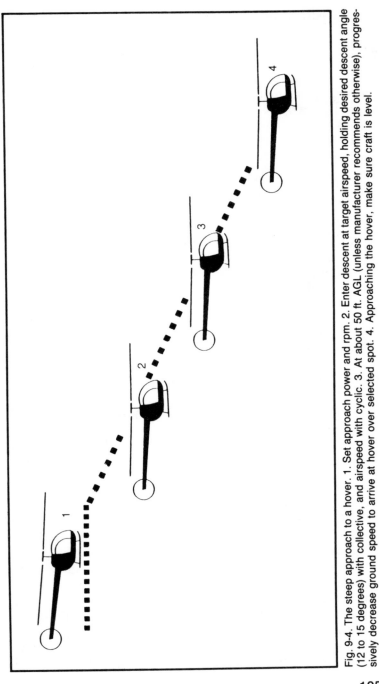

Fig. 9-4. The steep approach to a hover. 1. Set approach power and rpm. 2. Enter descent at target airspeed, holding desired descent angle (12 to 15 degrees) with collective, and airspeed with cyclic. 3. At about 50 ft. AGL (unless manufacturer recommends otherwise), progressively decrease ground speed to arrive at hover over selected spot. 4. Approaching the hover, make sure craft is level.

creased, left rudder pressure must be increased to maintain heading. Adjust throttle to keep proper rpm, and cyclic pitch is coordinated to control the change in forward airspeed.

Since the rate of descent on a steep approach is much higher than for normal approaches, the collective must be used much sooner at the bottom of the approach. The approach is terminated at hovering altitude above the intended landing point with zero ground speed. Very little, if any, additional power should be required to stop the forward movement and rate of descent of the helicopter if power has been properly applied during the final portion of the approach (Fig. 9-4).

Errors

- ☐ **Failure to maintain proper rpm during the entire approach.**
- ☐ **Improper use of collective in controlling the rate of descent.**
- ☐ **Failure to make pedal corrections to compensate for collective pitch changes during the approach.**
- ☐ **Slowing airspeed excessively in order to remain on the proper angle of descent.**
- ☐ **Failure to arrive at hovering altitude, hovering attitude, and zero ground speed almost simultaneously.**
- ☐ **Low rpm in transition to the hover at the end of the approach.**
- ☐ **Using too much rearward cyclic close to the ground,** which could result in the tail rotor striking the ground.

Landing from a Hover

In Chapter 6, how to take off to a hover was discussed. Here's its sequel—how to land vertically from a hover.

From an already attained hover, begin your descent by applying a slow, but gradual, downward pressure on the collective. Maintain a constant rate of descent to the ground. As the skids come to within a few feet of the surface, ground cushion effect becomes very noticeable, and the helicopter tends to stop its descent altogether. At this point, it may be necessary to further decrease the collective in order to maintain the constant rate of descent.

When the skids touch the ground, lower the collective to the full down position, adjust the throttle to keep rpm in the proper range, and at the same time add right pedal pressure as needed to maintain heading.

Throughout the descent and until the time the skids are firmly on the ground and the collective is in the full down position, make necessary corrections with rudders to keep a constant heading. Make the necessary cyclic corrections to hold a level attitude and to prevent movements over the ground.

Errors

☐ **Cyclic overcontrolling during descent,** resulting in movement over the ground on contact.

☐ **Failure to use collective smoothly.**

☐ **Pulling back on the cyclic prior to or upon touchdown.**

☐ **Failure to lower the collective smoothly and positively to the full down position upon ground contact.**

☐ **Failure to maintain a constant rate of descent.**

☐ **Failure to hold proper rpm.**

Shallow Approach and Running Landing

A shallow approach and running landing are used when a high density altitude or a high gross weight condition or a combination thereof is such that a normal or steep approach can't be made because of insufficient power to hover. To compensate for this lack of power, a shallow approach and running landing makes maximum use of translational lift until ground contact is made. The glide angle is from 5 to 12 degrees, depending on wind conditions. Since a running landing follows the shallow approach, a ground area of sufficient length and smoothness must be available.

Start the shallow approach in the same manner as a normal approach except that a shallower angle of descent is maintained. The power reduction to begin the desired angle of descent will be less than that for a normal approach, since the angle of descent is less. As collective is lowered, maintain heading by increasing right rud-

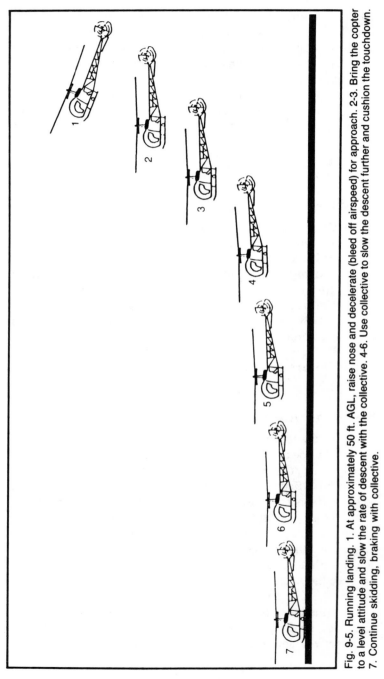

Fig. 9-5. Running landing. 1. At approximately 50 ft. AGL, raise nose and decelerate (bleed off airspeed) for approach. 2-3. Bring the copter to a level attitude and slow the rate of descent with the collective. 4-6. Use collective to slow the descent further and cushion the touchdown. 7. Continue skidding, braking with collective.

der pressure, adjust throttle to maintain rpm, and use cyclic as necessary to hold the desired approach airspeed.

As in normal and steep approaches, the descent angle and rate of descent are primarily controlled by collective, and the ground speed is primarily controlled by the cyclic. The coordination of all controls is needed, however, if the approach is to be accomplished successfully.

Approach airspeed should be held until reaching an altitude of approximately 50 feet AGL. At this point, gradually apply aft cyclic to start losing airspeed. Coordinate a slight downward pressure on the collective to maintain the proper descent angle. Airspeed deceleration should be enough that the helicopter will settle to the ground, due to the decreased effect of translational lift just as the landing spot is reached. Deceleration must be smoothly coordinated, at the same time keeping enough lift to prevent the copter from settling abruptly.

On final approach, prior to making ground contact, place the helicopter in a level attitude with cyclic, use rudder to maintain heading, and cyclic necessary to keep heading and ground track identical. Allow the helicopter to settle gently to the ground in a straight and level attitude, cushioning the landing with the collective.

After ground contact, the cyclic is placed slightly forward of neutral to tilt the main rotor away from the tail boom; adjust throttle to hold rpm; maintain ground track with cyclic. Normally, the collective is held stationary after touchdown until the helicopter comes to a complete stop. If braking action is desired or required, the collective may be lowered cautiously. To ensure directional control, normal rotor rpm must be maintained until the helicopter comes to a full stop (Fig. 9-5).

Errors

- [ ] **Assuming excessive nose-high attitude at about 10 feet.**
- [ ] **Insufficient collective and throttle to cushion the landing.**
- [ ] **Failure to add left rudder as collective is added to cushion landing,** resulting in a touchdown while in a left skid.
- [ ] **Touching down at an excessive ground speed.**

☐ Failure to touchdown in a level attitude.
☐ Failure to maintain proper rotor rpm during and after touchdown.
☐ Poor directional control upon touchdown.

10
Autorotations

One of the most frequently asked questions about helicopter flight is: What happens if the engine quits? The answer is, the helicopter enters the autorotational descent, in which air from below the rotor disc spins the rotor in pinwheel-like fashion, allowing a controlled descent to a landing.

Broadly speaking, in helicopter flying, an autorotation is a maneuver that you can perform whenever the engine is no longer supplying power to the main rotor blades. A chopper transmission is designed to allow the main rotor hub and its blades to rotate freely in its original direction if the engine stops.

Keep in mind that at the instant of engine failure, the blades will be producing lift and thrust. By immediately lowering the collective, lift, as well as drag, will be reduced. This will cause the craft to begin an immediate descent, thus producing an upward flow of air on the blades produces a ram effect which gives sufficient thrust to maintain rotor rpm throughout the descent. Since the tail rotor is driven by the main rotor during autorotation, heading control can still be maintained as if in normal flight.

Several factors affect the rate of descent in autorotation: density altitude, gross weight, rotor rpm, and airspeed. Your primary control of the rate of descent is airspeed. Higher or lower airspeed is obtained with the cyclic, just as in normal flight (Fig. 10-1).

You have a choice in angle of descent, varying from the vertical to maximum angle of descent or glide. Rate of descent is high

Fig. 10-1. In an autorotation from high altitude, the typical light helicopter (such as this Bell LongRanger) can safely "glide" one mile horizontally for every 1,000 foot of altitude loss.

at zero airspeed and decreases to a minimum somewhere in the neighborhood of 50 to 60 mph, depending on the particular copter and the factors just mentioned.

As the airspeed increases beyond that which gives you minimum rate of descent, the rate of your drop in altitude will again increase. When an autorotative landing is to be made, the energy stored in the rotating blades can be used to decrease the rate of descent even further and a safe landing made.

It should be emphasized that when a power failure occurs (whether simulated or actual), the pilot's first action should be to immediately lower the collective. Failure to do so will result in potentially dangerous rotor deceleration. In a helicopter with a high-inertia rotor system, such as the Enstrom F-28A, the pilot has a relatively long time to lower the collective; in the low-inertia-rotor helicopters, such as the Robinson R-22 or Hughes 269A, the pilot has only two or three seconds in which to react. There must be no hesitation. When a power failure is suspected, *lower the collective.*

A greater amount of rotor energy is required to stop the helicopter with a high rate of descent than one that is descending more slowly. It follows, then, that autorotative descents at very low or very high airspeeds are more critical than those performed at the proper airspeed for the minimum rate of descent.

Each type of helicopter has a specific airspeed at which a power-off glide is most efficient. The best airspeed is the one which combines the greatest glide range with the slowest rate of descent. The specified airspeed is somewhat different for each type of copter, yet certain factors affect all configurations in the same manner. For specific autorotation airpseeds for a particular helicopter, refer to that particular helicopter's flight manual.

The exact airspeed for autorotation is established for each type of helicopter on the basis of average weather and wind conditions and normal loading. When operating a machine with excessive loads in high density altitudes or strong, gusty wind conditions, best performance is achieved from a slightly increased airspeed in the descent. On the other hand, for autorotations in light winds, low density altitudes and light loading, best performance is achieved from a slightly decreased normal airspeed. Following this general procedure of fitting airspeed to existing conditions, you can achieve approximately the same glide angle in any set of circumstances and estimate the probable touchdown point.

When making autorotative turns, you should generally use cyclic control only. Use of rudder pedals to assist or speed the turn only causes loss of airspeed and downward pitching of the craft's nose; especially when left pedal is used. When autorotation is initiated, sufficient right rudder should be used to maintain straight flight and to prevent yawing to the left. Don't change this rudder pressure to assist the turn.

If rotor rpm becomes too high during an autorotative approach, collective should be raised sufficiently to decrease rpm to the normal operating range, then lowered all the way again. This procedure may be repeated as necessary to keep rpm in the normal mode.

Due to the increased back cyclic pressure, which induces a greater airflow through the rotor system, rpm is most likely to increase above the maximum limit during the turn. The tighter the turn and the heavier the gross weight, the higher the rpm will be.

Hovering Autorotation

To practice hovering autorotations, establish the normal hovering altitude for your particular helicopter, considering its load and the atmospheric conditions, and keep it headed into the wind, holding maximum allowable rpm.

To enter autorotation, close the throttle quickly to ensure a clean split of the engine and rotor needles. This disengages the driving force of the engine from the rotor, thus eliminating torque effect. As throttle is closed, right rudder pressure must be applied to maintain heading. Usually, a slight amount of right cyclic will be necessary to keep the craft from drifting, but use cyclic control as required to ensure a vertical descent and a level attitude. Leave the collective pitch where it is on entry.

In helicopters with low inertia rotor systems, the aircraft will begin to settle immediately. Keep a level attitude, and ensure a vertical descent with the cyclic heading with the rudders, and apply up collective pitch as necessary to slow the descent and cushion the landing (generally, the full amount of collective is required). As upward collective is applied, the throttle will have to be held in the closed position to prevent the rotor from re-engaging.

Machines with high inertia rotor systems will maintain altitude momentarily after the throttle is closed. As rotor rpm decreases, the craft will start to settle. As it does so, apply upward collective, while holding the throttle in the closed position to slow the descent and cushion the landing. The timing of this collective application, and the rate at which it is applied, depends on the particular helicopter being flown, its gross weight and the atmospheric conditions. Use cyclic to maintain a level attitude and to ensure a vertical descent. Keep heading with rudders.

When the weight of the helicopter is entirely on the skids, stop application of up collective. When the craft has come to a complete stop, lower the collective completely.

The timing of the collective is a most important consideration. If it's applied too soon, the remaining rpm will not be sufficient to effect a smooth landing. On the other hand, if collective is initiated too late, ground contact will be made before sufficient blade pitch is increased to cushion the landing ground contact. Avoid landing on the heels of the skid gear. The timing of the collective application, and the amount applied, will be dependent on the rate of descent.

After ground contact is made, collective may be increased smoothly (still holding the throttle in the closed position), to keep the helicopter light on the skids and allow it to slow down gradually; or it may be held stationary, resulting in a shorter ground run; or it may be lowered cautiously for additional braking, if required, due to a fast touchdown and limited landing area. Hold cyclic slightly forward of neutral and use to keep directional control if landing is made in a crosswind. Maintain heading with rudders. In the event of insufficient rudder travel to maintain heading con-

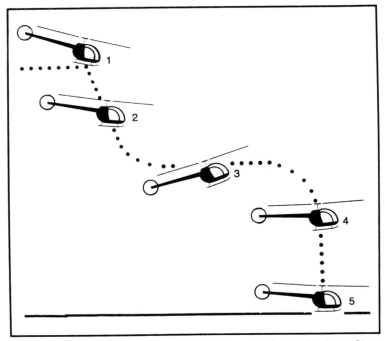

Fig. 10-2. Autorotation after engine failure. 1. Lower collective full-down. Close the throttle completely to "split the needles." 2. Maintain directional control with pedals and use the cyclic to establish recommended autorotation speed (usually around 50 mph). 3. Flare with cyclic to decelerate the aircraft to a safe touchdown speed. 4-5. Move the cyclic forward to level the helicopter, and use the collective to cushion the touchdown.

trol when the rotor rpm decreases after touchdown, apply cyclic in the direction of the turn (Fig. 10-2).

After the helicopter has stopped, decrease collective to the full down position. If a power recovery is to be made from the practice approach, replace certain of the above procedures with those found in "Power Recovery from Practice Autorotation," found in this chapter.

Errors

- [ ] **Failure to use sufficient right rudder when power is reduced.**
- [ ] **Lowering the noise too abruptly when power is reduced,** thus placing the craft in a dive.
- [ ] **Failure to maintain full down collective during the descent.**
- [ ] **Application of up collective at an excessive altitude,** resulting in a hard landing, loss of heading control and, possibly, damage to the tail rotor and main rotor blade stops.
- [ ] **Pulling the nose up just prior to touchdown.**

Flare Autorotation

This maneuver enables you to land at any speed between a no landing run to that of a running one—that is to say, anywhere between a zero ground speed and the speed of touchdown from a no-flare autorotation. The speed at touchdown and the resulting ground run will depend on the rate and amount of the flare: The greater the degree of flare and the longer it is held, the slower the touchdown speed and the shorter the ground run. The slower the speed desired at touchdown from an autorotation, the more accurate must be the timing and speed of the flare, especially in craft with low inertia rotor systems.

Enter the flare autorotation in the same manner as the no-flare autorotation. The technique is the same down to the point where the flare is to begin. This point is slightly lower than the point at which the noise is raised in the no-flare autorotation.

At approximately 35 to 60 feet AGL, depending on the particular helicopter (check the manufacturer's recommendation), initiate the flare by moving the cyclic smoothly to the rear. Heading is maintained by the rudders. Care must be exercised in the execution of the flare so the cyclic isn't moved rearward so abruptly as to cause the helicopter to climb or so slowly as to allow it to settle so rapidly that the tail rotor strikes the ground.

As forward motion decreases to the desired ground speed, move the cyclic forward to a level attitude in preparation for landing. If a landing is to be made, rotate the throttle to the closed or override position. If power recovery is to be made, do so as the copter reaches the level position.

The altitude at this time should be about 3 to 10 feet, depending on the helicopter. If a landing is to be made, allow the craft to settle vertically. Apply collective smoothly as necessary to check the descent and cushion the landing. As collective pitch is increased, hold the throttle in the closed position so that the rotor will not re-engage. Additional right rudder is required to maintain heading, as collective is raised, due to the reduction in motor rpm and the resulting reduced effect of the tail rotor.

After touchdown, when the chopper has come to a complete stop, lower the collective to the full down position.

Errors

- ☐ **Failure to use sufficient right rudder when power is reduced.**
- ☐ **Lowering the noise too abruptly when power is reduced,** thus placing the craft in a dive.
- ☐ **Failure to maintain full down collective during the descent.**
- ☐ **Application of up collective at an excessive altitude,** resulting in a hard landing, loss of heading control, and possible damage to the tail rotor and the main rotor blade stops.
- ☐ **Applying up collective before a level attitude is attained:** If timing is late, it may be necessary to apply up collective before a level attitude is attained.
- ☐ **Pulling the nose up just prior to touchdown on full autorotation.**

Power Recovery from Practice Autorotations

A power recovery is used to terminate practice autorotations at a point prior to actual touchdown. If so desired, a landing can be made or a go-around initiated after the power recovery is made.

To effect a power recovery after the flare or level-off, coordinate upward collective and increase throttle to join the needles at operating rpm. The throttle and collective must be coordinated properly. If the throttle is increased too fast or too much, an engine overspeed will occur. If the throttle is increased too slow or too little in proportion to the increase in collective, a loss of rotor rpm will result. Use sufficient collective to check the descent, and coordinate left rudder with the increase in collective to maintain heading.

If a go-around is to be made, move the cyclic control smoothly forward to re-enter forward flight. If a landing is to be made following the power recovery, the helicopter can be brought to a hover at normal hovering altitude.

In transitioning from a practice autorotation to a go-around, care must be exercised to avoid an altitude-airspeed combination that could place the craft in an unsafe area of the height-velocity chart for that particular helicopter.

Errors

- ☐ **Initiating recovery too late**, requiring a rapid application of controls, resulting in overcontrolling.
- ☐ **Failure to obtain and maintain a level attitude near the ground.**
- ☐ **Adding throttle before the collective.**
- ☐ **Failure to coordinate throttle and collective properly,** resulting in an engine overspeed or loss of rpm.
- ☐ **Failure to coordinate left rudder with the increase in power.**

11

Practice Maneuvers

The purpose of practice maneuvers is to build coordination and to keep you familiar with your aircraft and your own skill level. They give you the opportunity to practice many single maneuvers in one, by grouping them as a single unit. They also instill an automatic reflex to certain configurations (Fig. 11-1).

Two major practice maneuvers are the S-turns and rapid deceleration or "quick-stop."

S-Turns

This single maneuver presents one of the most elementary problems in the practical application of a turn, and also for wind correction or drift while in a turn. To set up for S-turns, a reference line is used. This line can be a road, railroad, fence or section line; however, it should be straight for a considerable distance. It should extend as nearly perpendicular to the wind as possible.

The objective of the S-turn is to fly a pattern of two half-circle of equal size on opposite sides of a reference line. The maneuver should be started at an altitude of about 500 feet AGL and flown at a constant altitude above the terrain throughout. S-turns may be started at any point; however, during early training, it may be beneficial to start on a downwind heading.

As your helicopter crosses the reference line, a bank is immediately established. This initial bank will be the steepest used through-

Fig. 11-1. In ag operations, the ability to maneuver safely in confined spaces is paramount. Practice maneuvers such as tree-topping can be beneficial to maintain top proficiency.

out the maneuver since the craft is headed directly downwind. The bank is gradually reduced as necessary to scribe a ground track in a half-circle. The turn should be timed so that as the rollout is completed, the helicopter is crossing the reference line, perpendicular to it and headed directly upwind.

A bank is immediately entered in the opposite direction to begin the second half of the S-turn. Since the copter is on an upwind heading, this, as well as the one just completed before crossing the reference line, will be the shallowest in the maneuver. The turn should gradually be increased as necessary to scribe a ground track which is a half-circle identical in size to the one previously completed on the other side of the reference line. The steepest bank in this turn should be attained just prior to rollout when the craft is approaching the reference line nearest to a downwind heading. This bank, along with the initial bank entered at the beginning of the maneuver, will be the steepest bank used in S-turns. The turn should be timed so that as the rollout is completed, the helicopter is crossing the reference line perpendicular to it and headed directly downwind.

From here, the maneuver can be started over again without

breaking the pattern. It can be continued as long as the reference line runs true without a break. You can do a number in one direction, then do a 180-degree turn and head back along the same track in the direction from which you just came.

As a summary, the angle of bank required at any given point in the maneuver is dependent on the ground speed—the faster the ground speed, the steeper the bank of the turn. Or, to express it another way, the more nearly the helicopter is to a downwind heading, the steeper the bank; the more nearly it is to an upwind heading, the shallower the bank.

In addition to varying the angle of bank to correct for wind drift in order to maintain the proper radius of turn, the chopper must also be flown with a drift correction angle (crab) in relation to its ground track, except, of course, when it's on direct upwind or downwind headings, or there's no wind. You would normally think of the fore and aft axes of the craft as being tangent to the ground track pattern at each point, however, this isn't the case.

During the turn on the upwind side of the reference line (the side from which the wind is blowing), the nose of the helicopter will be crabbed toward the outside of the circle. During the turn on the downwind side of the reference line (the side opposite to the direction from which the wind is blowing), the nose of the helicopter will be crabbed toward the inside of the circle. In any case, the craft will be crabbed into the wind, just as if trying to maintain a straight ground track. The amount of crab depends on the wind speed and how close the ship is to its crosswind position. The higher the wind speed, the greater the crab angle at any given position for a scribed turn of a specific radius. The closer the helicopter is to a crosswind position, the greater the crab angle. The maximum crab angle should be at the point of each half-circle farthest from the reference line (Fig. 11-2).

Standard radius for S-turns cannot be specified. This radius will depend on the airspeed of the helicopter, velocity of the wind and the initial bank angle required for the entry.

Errors

☐ **Failure to maintain two half-circles of equal distance from the reference line.**

☐ **Too much or too little crab for crosswind.**

☐ **Sloppy coordination on the controls.**

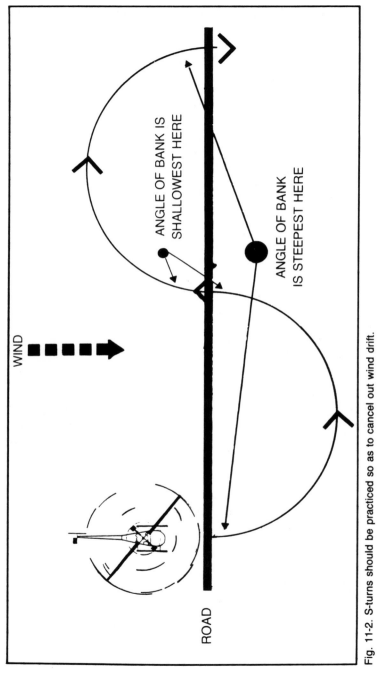

WIND

ANGLE OF BANK IS SHALLOWEST HERE

ANGLE OF BANK IS STEEPEST HERE

ROAD

Fig. 11-2. S-turns should be practiced so as to cancel out wind drift.

☐ **Failure to cross reference line in level flight attitude.**

☐ **Loss or gain in altitude during maneuver.**

Quick Stops

Although used primarily for coordination practice, decelerations can be used to effect a quick stop in the air. The purpose of such a maneuver is to maintain a constant heading, altitude, and rpm, while slowing the helicopter to a desired ground speed. It requires a high degree of coordination of all controls. It should be practiced at an altitude that will permit a safe clearance between tail rotor and the ground, especially at the point where the pitch attitude is highest. Telephone pole height should be sufficient, depending on type of craft flown. The altitude at completion should be no higher than the maximum, hovering altitude prescribed by the manufacturer. In selecting an altitude to begin the maneuver, the overall length of the helicopter and its height-velocity chart must be considered.

Although the maneuver is called a rapid deceleration or "quick stop," this doesn't mean that it should necessarily be used through the completion. The rate of deceleration is at your discretion, but blade G factors must be taken into consideration. A quick stop is completed when the helicopter comes to a hover during the recovery.

Begin the maneuver at a fast hover taxi speed, headed into the wind. An altitude should be selected that's high enough to avoid danger to the tail rotor during the flare, but low enough to stay out of the craft's shaded area throughout the maneuver, and also low enough that it can be brought to a hover during the recovery.

To start, decrease collective, simultaneously increasing rearward pressure on the cyclic. This rearward movement of the stick must be exactly timed to the lowering of the collective. If rearward cyclic is applied too fast, the craft will start to climb; if rearward cyclic is applied too slowly, the chopper will descend. The faster the decrease in collective, the more rapid should be the increase in rearward stick pressure, and the faster will be the deceleration. As collective is lowered, right rudder should be increased to maintain heading, and the throttle should be adjusted to maintain rpm.

Once speed has been reduced to the desired amount, recovery is initiated by lowering the nose and allowing the helicopter to settle to a normal hovering altitude, in level flight and zero ground speed or that desired.

During recovery, collective pitch should be increased as necessary to stop the craft at normal hovering altitude; throttle should be adjusted to maintain rpm; and left pedal pressure should be increased as necessary to maintain heading (Fig. 11-3).

Errors

☐ **Failure to lead slightly with down collective on the entry.**

☐ **Failure to raise the nose high enough**, resulting in slow deceleration.

☐ **Applying back cyclic too rapidly initially**, causing the helicopter to "balloon," gaining altitude suddenly.

☐ **Failure to lead with, and maintain, forward cyclic during recovery.** If a quick stop isn't performed properly, it may be necessary to lead with collective, to prevent touching down too hard or on the heels of the skids.

☐ **Allowing the helicopter to stop forward motion in a tail-low attitude.**

☐ **Failure to maintain proper rpm.**

Tree Topper

This maneuver is another coordination stratagem—one to practice using all controls in making minute corrections, while enjoying yourself. It's much like the S-turn in that wind correction is involved.

Pick a wide-open area with a tree, pole or some object in the middle. Make sure there's good all around clearance. The objective is to look the chosen object over by moving your craft around it, as well as up and down.

To start the maneuver, approach the object slowly from upwind at about hovering altitude. An upwind entry is desired to get the feel of wind speed and what it takes to stop short of the object.

Move to the object, being extremely careful not to touch it with blade tips. Notice your blade clearance. Move the helicopter lower and lower, gradually, making corrections with collective, cyclic, rudder and throttle. You should be moving forward, around the object, at the same time.

Once this has been done, move higher and higher, looking the object over. Again, extreme care should be used in keeping the blades away from the object. Make necessary corrections on the

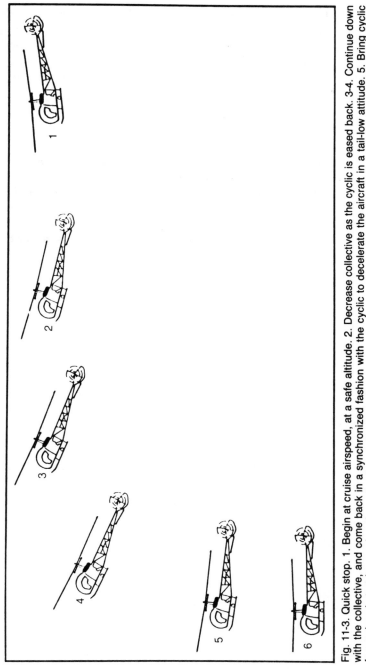

Fig. 11-3. Quick stop. 1. Begin at cruise airspeed, at a safe altitude. 2. Decrease collective as the cyclic is eased back. 3-4. Continue down with the collective, and come back in a synchronized fashion with the cyclic to decelerate the aircraft in a tail-low attitude. 5. Bring cyclic forward and start increasing the collective. 6. Follow through with a normal hover landing.

controls to keep the craft moving at a steady pace, keeping your distance from the object.

Once you've made a trip or two around it, and you have the feel of both the machine and wind, coordinating the controls, find another object and try the whole sequence over. Remember, caution is the word.

Errors

☐ **Failure to take into account the effect of wind as you move around the object.**

☐ **Failure to coordinate controls with changes in collective, rpm, and rudder as you move up and down and around the object.**

☐ **Failure to keep an equal distance from the object as the craft moves around it.** An equal-radius circle should be scribed on the ground.

12
Emergency Procedures

Since emergency procedures differ with particular aircraft, before simulating any emergency, you should check the manufacturer's recommendations. There are, however, certain general emergency steps that every helicopter pilot should be familiar with, no matter what type of copter is being flown. It's the purpose of this chapter to acquaint you with this information.

Recovery from Low Rotor RPM

The recovery from low rotor rpm procedure is used to return the rotor to normal operating rpm. This technique is often referred to as *milking*. If performed properly, it will normally regain lost rotor rpm while still maintaining level flight. The low rotor rpm condition is the result of having a high angle of attack on the main rotor blades, induced by too much collective. It creates a drag so great that engine power available, or power being used, isn't sufficient to maintain normal rotor operating rpm.

When you realize what's happening, immediately add full throttle and briskly decrease the collective to relieve—momentarily at least—the excess engine load. (This is one of very few times in which it is appropriate to make a rapid and dramatic throttle change.) As the helicopter begins to settle, smoothly increase the collective, but only enough to stop the settling motion. Remember, down briskly; up smoothly and slower. This procedure, under critical conditions, might have to be repeated several times in order to regain normal rotor operating rpm. The amount that the collective can be decreased will depend on the altitude available at the time of the emergency condition. In practice, give yourself plenty of room to spare.

When operating at sufficient altitudes above the terrain, it will be necessary to decrease the collective only once to regain sufficient rotor rpm. When the rotor rpm begins to rise and attains about normal rotor operating rpm, anticipate decreasing the throttle slowly to prevent the engine from overspeeding.

If recovery from a low rotor rpm condition isn't effected soon enough, lifting power of the main rotor blades will be lost, as will rudder control.

This pedal control loss occurs as a result of the decrease in tail rotor rpm. Remember, the tail rotor is driven by the main rotor, and its rpm is directly proportional to that of the main rotor. If rudder control is lost and the altitude is such that a landing can be effected before the turning rate increases dangerously, decrease collective pitch slowly, maintain a level attitude with the cyclic and land.

Recovery from Blade Stall

Blade stall occurs when, at a high forward speed, the angle of attack of the retreating blade is made so acute that the streamline flow of air over its upper surface, especially toward blade tip, reaches the burbling point and begins breaking down. Each blade will stall when it becomes the retreating blade. The high angle of attack can also be increased beyond the critical angle and cause complete blade stall, as in such maneuvers as a steep turn or sudden up-gusts of air. Again, the airspeed at which blade stall commences will be reduced when the craft has a high, all-up weight or when it's at high altitudes, as a greater degree of collective must be used in these conditions (Fig. 12-1).

You will first feel blade stall as a vibration equivalent to the number of blades in the main rotor, per revolution. That is to say, a three-bladed rotor will have three vibrations per revolution, two-blades will have two, and so forth. The vibration can be fairly severe and a kicking at the controls can be present.

When blade stall occurs, you can correct the situation by reducing the severity of the maneuver, reduce collective pitch, reduce airspeed/and increase rotor rpm, or combination thereof. It depends on your situation at the time.

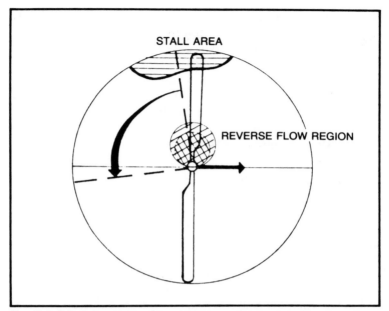

Fig. 12-1. Retreating blade stall occurs from the outboard end of the retreating blade in, and from the inboard end out.

A blade stall which is encountered because of the severity of a maneuver will normally correct itself, as soon as you reduce the harshness of, or cease entirely, the maneuver. This is applicable if the blade stall occurs in a steep turn, a sharp pull out at a high speed, etc.

In the majority of blade stall cases, reducing collective pitch is the right action, especially when flying fast in turbulent weather. In copters that are prone to high speed stalling of advancing blades (usually due to their reaching a high, critical, mach number), it's possible not to know which of the two possible causes is producing the vibrations felt. A slight reduction in rpm would, therefore, be advisable at the same time as the collective is lowered.

There's some debate against an immediate reduction of airspeed in the case of a blade stall at high cruising speed. Some feel the result of easing back on the cyclic would be to increase the G load and further aggravate stall symptoms. It's recommended that a reduction of airspeed should be accomplished slowly, and the collective should be lowered at the same time.

If higher rotor rpm can be used with a lower collective setting, then blade stall will occur at a higher cruising speed. In some helicopters, the possibility of reach critical mach numbers with the advancing blades must be kept in mind when rpm is increased.

Much depends upon the type of helicopter being used as to the manner in which blade stall is induced. With some craft, blade-stall onset could be experienced frequently during routing exercises, however, in others extreme steep turns, with high G effects at attitude, may have to be carried out before blade stall is encountered.

Vortex Ring Condition (Settling with Power)

This situation can occur during a vertical descent through the air with power on, with a rate of descent in excess of 300 fpm usually being necessary. Although less common, it can also occur in conditions where considerable power is applied, with the helicopter mushing through the disturbed air. The latter case is generally only momentary but can cause considerable buffeting and a loss of lift (Fig. 12-2).

In the case of the vertical descent, the effect can be prolonged, resulting in a high rate of descent, vibration and partial loss of control. The symptoms may vary among different helicopter types.

The vortex ring isn't dangerous, unless carried out at a low altitude. The rate of descent is high, both during the condition and recovery. Altitude should therefore not be held deliberately below 600 feet AGL. Steep or vertical approaches to small sites in calm air should be carried out at a low rate of descent in order to avoid the vortex ring condition.

This problem is so named because of the airflow pattern around the rotor. From the pilot's point of view, it may be thought of more simply as the fact that the rotor is forcing air downward, and the aircraft is then sinking into this downward-moving, disturbed air. It's not always easy to initiate the condition for demonstration purposes, as sideways, forward or backward movement through the air could prevent its occurring.

When the condition is encountered in a vertical descent, there are two main ways of recovery:

☐ Easing the stick forward and diving out.
☐ Entering autorotation; placing the collective full down and diving out.

Engine Failure

This emergency can happen any time, any place. It should be

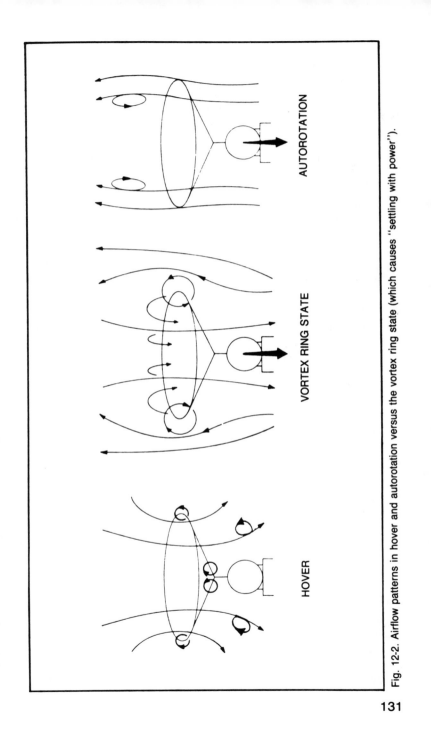

HOVER   VORTEX RING STATE   AUTOROTATION

Fig. 12-2. Airflow patterns in hover and autorotation versus the vortex ring state (which causes "settling with power").

kept foremost in mind and a precautionary landing made any time there's indication of engine trouble. It's better to land with some power than none at all. Obviously, the most critical time for an engine out would be when working close to the ground in such attitudes as takeoff, landing, or a low hover.

If time and altitude permit when engine failure occurs, rapidly reduce the main rotor's pitch with the collective a proportional amount to your altitude AGL. At an altitude of 300 feet and up, say, reduce collective to the maximum, which will reduce the rotor blade's pitch to a minimum. At altitudes of 10 feet or less, reduce the collective only a slight amount, if at all.

If altitude permits, obtain some forward airspeed. Transition to a forward glide advantageously reduces the rate of descent. From here, a normal landing without power can be made.

At an altitude of 5 to 10 feet AGL, rapidly increase the main rotor's pitch angle with the collective, depending on your rate of descent. You should make every effort to utilize all available rotor energy to cushion the landing. However, you should save some collective for the last few feet before touchdown.

If you're above 50 feet AGL, instantly execute an autorotative glide by applying appropriate forward cyclic and maximum down collective. This will permit the copter to descend along a forward path at complementary forward speed.

When approaching normal hovering altitude, apply backward cyclic to flare. This will reduce forward speed and further decrease the rate of descent. At about head high, 5 to 8 feet AGL, level the flare enough to bring the helicopter to an almost level attitude. A final cushioning effect with increased rotor blade pitch by up collective at approximately 2 to 4 feet AGL. This should set the craft nicely on the chosen spot.

After touchdown, turn battery switch, selector valve and ignition switch to the "off" position. Also place the mixture control in the "cut-off" position. Climb out of the craft, and you're home free.

Tail Rotor Control System Failure

Failure of the tail rotor is one of the more dangerous of helicopter emergencies, but if you're ready for it, for immediate action, it's just another emergency maneuver. Since it controls the directional stability of the craft, without the tail rotor, there's a tendency of the helicopter to begin turning in the opposite direction of the rotor blades, causing a landing or inflight problem, if forward speed gets too low.

Immediately go into an autorotative attitude and maintain an airspeed sufficient to keep the craft aligned parallel with its forward ground track. Make an autorotational landing, while heading in a direction that's parallel to the flight or glide path. A "running landing" here would be most appropriate—enough so to keep the tail from swinging around.

Antitorque system failure could be the result of a failure in the tail rotor blades, the mechanical linkage between the rudders and the pitch-change mechanism of the tail rotor or the tail rotor driveshaft between the transmission and the tail rotor.

If the system fails in cruising flight, the nose of the helicopter will usually pitch slightly and yaw to the right. The direction in which the nose pitches will depend on your particular craft and how it's loaded. Violence in pitching and yawing is generally greater when the failure occurs in the tail rotor blades and also is usually accompanied by severe vibration.

Pitching and yawing can be overcome by holding the cyclic stick near neutral and immediately entering autorotation. Keep cyclic movements to a minimum until the pitching subsides. Abrupt rearward movements of the cyclic should be avoided. If the stick is moved rearward too fast, the main rotor blades could flex downward with sufficient force to strike the tail boom.

The fuselage will remain fairly well streamlined if sufficient forward speed is maintained. However, if you attempt a descent at slow speeds, a continuous turning movement to the left can be expected. Know the manufacturer's recommended speeds and procedures for each particular helicopter you fly. This will generally be found under "Emergency Procedures" in the aircraft flight manual. Directional control should be maintained primarily with cyclic and secondarily by gently applying throttle momentarily, with needles joined, to swing the nose to the right.

A running landing may be made or a flare-type. The best, and safest, landing technique, terrain permitting, is to land directly into the wind with about 20 mph airspeed. In a flare landing, the helicopter will turn to the left during the actual flare and subsequent vertical descent. An important factor to remember is that the craft should be level, or approximately level, at ground contact, in any case.

Immediate and quick action must be taken. The turning motion to the right builds up rapidly, because of the torque reaction produced by the relatively high power setting. To eliminate the turning effect, you should close the throttle immediately without varying collective pitch. Simultaneously, adjust the cyclic to stop all sideward or rearward movements and to level the chopper for touchdown. From this point, the procedure for a hovering autorotation is followed.

Low-Frequency Vibrations

Abnormal, low-frequency vibrations are always associated with the main rotor. These vibrations will be at some frequency related to the rotor rpm and the number of blades of the rotor, such as one vibration per rotor revolution, two per rev, three per rev, etc. Low frequency vibrations are slow enough that they can be counted.

The frequency and strength of the vibrations will cause you and/or your passengers to be noticeably bounced or shaken. If the vibration is felt through the cyclic, it'll have some definite kick at the same point in the rotor-blade cycle. These low-frequency vibrations can be felt in the fuselage, in the stick, or they can be evident in all simultaneously. Whether the tremor is in the fuselage or the stick will, to some extent, determine the cause.

Vibrations felt through the fuselage can be classified in four ways: *lateral, longitudinal, vertical* or a *combination* of the others. A lateral vibration is one which throws the pilot from side-to-side. A longitudinal vibration is one which rocks the pilot forward-and-backward, or in which the pilot receives a periodic kick in the back. A vertical vibration is one in which the pilot is bounced up-and-down, or it may be thought of as one in which the pilot receives a periodic "kick in the seat of the pants." Describing the vibrations to a mechanic in the above forms will also help him in determining the exact cause.

Vibrations felt through both the stick and fuselage are generally indicative of problems in the rotor or rotor support. A failure of the pylon support at the fuselage connection is also a possible cause.

If the low-frequency vibration in the fuselage occurs during translational flight or during a climb at certain airspeeds, the vibration could be a result of the blades striking their rest stops. This problem can be eliminated until mechanical correction by avoiding the flight conditions that cause it.

For low-frequency vibrations felt predominantly through the stick, the trouble is most likely in the control system linkage, from the stick to the rotor head.

Medium-Frequency Vibrations

In most helicopters, medium-frequency vibrations are a result of trouble with the tail rotor. Improper rigging, unbalance, defective blades or bad bearings in the tail rotor are all sources of this type vibrations. If it occurs only during turns, the trouble could be caused by insufficient tail-rotor flapping action. Medium-frequency vibrations are very difficult, if not impossible, to count, due to their first rate. See a mechanic for a thorough checkout.

High-Frequency Vibrations

These vibrations are associated with the engine in most helicopters and will be impossible to count, due to their high rate. However, they could be associated with the tail rotor in helicopters with tail rotor rpm about equal to, or greater than engine rpm. A defective clutch or missing or bent fan blade will cause vibrations. Any bad bearing in the engine, transmission or tail rotor drive shaft will result in vibrations with frequencies directly related to the speed of the engine.

Experience in detecting and isolating the three main different classes of vibrations when they first develop makes it possible to correct the situation long before it becomes serious. Take a good look, feel and listen. If you don't like what you find, see a mechanic.

Engine Overspeed

Engine overspeed is a condition in which the aircraft engine is inadvertently revved beyond the redline marking on the tachometer. (In a piston helicopter, this means operating beyond approximately 3,000 rpm.) An overspeed is potentially dangerous since it subjects reciprocating parts—connecting rods, rod bolts, cam lobes, and valves in particular—to stress loads for which they were not engineered. Operation at rpms greater than 100 percent of redline for periods of more than 20 seconds can necessitate a costly engine teardown inspection.

Overspeeds are usually the result of pilot carelessness in recovering from a rapid descent, quick stop, or other abrupt maneuver; it results from failure to *make all throttle adjustments gradual in nature*. When "rolling on" the throttle, remember to do so smoothly and slowly at all times.

Occasionally, overspeeds are due to factors beyond the pilot's control. Hard to believe as it may sound, there are cases on record of passengers departing the helicopter's left seat after landing, and sliding across the collective's twist-grip throttle, revving the engine beyond redline. If you fly your ship from the right seat, be sure to instruct passengers on how to exit the aircraft without "rolling open" the throttle.

13

Special Operations

A special operation is one that is out of the ordinary. Such an operation would include flight in confined areas, high, low, and ground reconnaissance maneuvers.

Slope Operations

Approaching a slope, mountain, hill, or knoll for landing isn't much different from an approach to any other helicopter landing area. However, during this type of operation, an allowance must be made for wind, obstacles, and a possible forced landing. Since the terrain incline could constitute a barrier to the wind, turbulence and downdrafts must be anticipated because of air spilling over and down.

It's usually best to land the helicopter cross-slope rather than upslope. And, landing downslope or downhill is definitely *not* recommended because of the possibility of striking the tail rotor on the ground during normal flare out.

Maneuver slowly toward the incline, being especially careful not to turn the tail upslope. The helicopter should be hovered in a position cross-slope, directly over the spot of intended landing.

A slight downward pressure on the collective will put the copter in a slow descent. As the upslope skid touches the ground, apply cyclic pressure in the direction of the slope. This will hold the skid against the incline, while you continue a gradual letdown with the collective (Fig. 13-1).

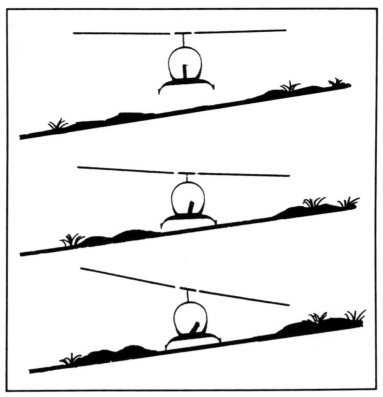

Fig. 13-1. Slope landing and takeoff.

As collective is reduced, continue to move the cyclic toward the slope as needed to maintain a fixed position. The slope must be shallow enough to allow you to hold the craft against it with the cyclic during the entire landing.

A five-degree slope is considered maximum for normal operation of most helicopters. Each make of machine will generally let you know in its own particular way when you're about to run out of lateral cyclic, such as the rotor hub hitting the rotor mast, vibrations felt through the cyclic, etc. If you encounter such warnings, don't land. They indicate the slope is too steep for safe operations.

Once the downslope skid has touched the ground, continue to lower the collective until reaching the stop. Maintain normal rotor operating rpm until the full weight of the chopper rests on the skids. This will assure adequate rotor rpm for immediate takeoff if the craft should start to slide downhill. Use the rudders as necessary throughout the landing to maintain heading.

Extreme case must be exercised in making slope landings to ensure that a *dynamic rollover* does not occur. Dynamic rollover is the name given to a condition in which the rotorcraft (by touching one skid too low, or—more commonly—touching with some sideways velocity, causing a skid to "dig in") tilts so much to one side that no amount of cyclic control can effect a recovery, and the helicopter continues to keel over until it strikes a rotor blade on the ground. Dynamic rollover is more apt to occur with a two-bladed, teetering-rotor helicopter (such as Bell JetRanger or Hiller UH-12) than with a three-bladed-rotor helicopter such as the Hughes 269A or Enstrom F-28. This is due to the greater measure of controllability offered by the offset flapping hinge design employed in the latter copters. (However, hitting the ground hard on one skid in a three-bladed helicopter is apt to induce ground resonance, so no matter what kind of ship you fly, it is wise to approach slope landings with extreme caution.)

The procedure for a slope takeoff is almost the exact reverse of that for a slope landing. Adjust the throttle to obtain takeoff rotor rpm and slowly move the cyclic in the direction of the slope so that the rotor rotation plane is parallel to the true horizontal rather than the slope. Apply up-collective smoothly. As the helicopter becomes light on the skids, apply rudders as needed to maintain heading.

Upon raising the downslope skid and the helicopter approaches a level attitude, return the cyclic to the neutral position. Continue to apply up collective, taking the craft straight up to a hover, before moving away from the slope. As you depart, care should be taken that the tail doesn't turn upslope. Remember the danger of the tail rotor striking the ground.

Errors

- ☐ **Failure to maintain proper rotor rpm throughout the entire maneuver.**
- ☐ **Letting the craft down too rapidly.**
- ☐ **Failure to adjust cyclic to keep the craft from sliding downhill.**

Confined Area Operations

A *confined area* is a locale where the flight of your helicopter is limited in some direction by terrain or the presence of obstructions, natural or manmade: a clearing in the woods, a city street, a road, a building roof, etc. (Fig. 13-2).

Barriers on the ground, or the ground itself, can interfere with the smooth flow of air, resulting in turbulence. This interference is transmitted to upper air levels as larger, but less, intense disturbances. Therefore the greatest turbulence is usually found at low altitudes. Gusts are unpredictable variations in wind velocity. Ordinary gusts are dangerous only in slow flight at very low altitudes. You might be unaware of such a gust. Its cessation could reduce airspeed below that required to sustain flight, due to the loss of effective translational lift. Gusts cannot be planned for or anticipated. Turbulence, however, can generally be predicted. You'll find turbulence in the following areas, when wind velocity exceeds 10 mph:

☐ Near the ground on the downwind side of trees, buildings, hills or other obstructions. The turbulence area is always relative in size to that of the obstacle, and relative in intensity to the speed of the wind.

☐ Near the ground on the immediate upwind side of any solid obstacle, such as trees in leaf and buildings. This condition isn't generally dangerous, unless the wind velocity is 15 knots or higher.

☐ In the air, above and slightly downwind of any sizable obstruction, such as a hill or mountain range. The size of the obstruction and the wind speed govern the height to which the turbulence extends and also its severity.

You should know the direction and approximate speed of the wind at all times. Plan landings and takeoffs with the wind conditions in mind. This doesn't necessarily mean that takeoffs and landings should always be made into the wind, but wind must be considered, and its velocity will, many times, determine proper avenues on approach and takeoff.

In case of engine failure, plan flights over areas suitable for forced landing, if possible. You might find it necessary to choose between a crosswind approach over an open area and one directly into the wind but over heavily wooded or extremely rough terrain where a safe forced landing would be impossible. Perhaps the initial approach phase can be made crosswind over the open area, and then it may be possible to execute a turn into the wind for the final approach portion.

Fig. 13-2. Pinnacle-landing skills are called for to operate safely off an oil rig platform; there is no room for error. (Shown here is a Sikorsky S-76 twin-jet helicopter.)

Always operate the copter as closely to its normal capabilities as possible while considering the situation at hand. In all confined areas operations, with the exception of the pinnacle operation, of course, the angle of descent should be no steeper than is necessary to clear any barrier in the avenue of approach and still land on the pre-selected spot. The angle of climb on takeoff shouldn't be any steeper than is necessary to clear any barrier. It's far better to clear the barrier by just a few feet and maintain normal rotor operating rpm with, perhaps, a reserve of power, than it is to clear the obstruction by a wide margin but with dangerously low rotor rpm and no power reserve.

Always make the landing to a specific point and not to just some general area. The more confined the area, the more essential it is that you land the helicopter precisely on a definite point. Keep this spot in sight during the entire final approach phase.

Any increase in elevation between the point of takeoff and the point of intended landing must be given due consideration, because sufficient power must be available to bring the chopper to a hover at the point of the intended landing. A decrease in wind speed should also be allowed for with the presence of obstructions.

If you're flying a helicopter near obstructions, it's critical that you consider the tail rotor. Therefore, a safe angle of descent over barriers must be established to ensure tail into obstructions.

Make a high reconnaissance to determine the suitability of the area for a landing. In a high reconnaissance, the following items should be accomplished:

1. Determine wind direction and speed.
2. Select the most suitable flight paths in and out of the area, with particular consideration being given a forced landing.
3. Plan the approach and select a touchdown point.
4. Locate and determine the size of obstacles immediately around the chosen area.

A high reconnaissance is flown at about 500 feet AGL, however, a higher altitude may be required in some craft.

Always ensure sufficient altitude to land into the wind in case of engine failure. This means the greatest altitude will be required when you're headed downwind. If possible, make a complete circle of the area. A 45-degree angle of observation will generally allow you to best analyze the presence and height of obstacles, the size of the area, and the slope of the terrain. Safe altitudes and airspeed should be maintained, and a forced landing area should be kept within reach. This point can't be overemphasized.

Your approach path should generally be into the wind and over terrain that minimizes the time that you're out of reach of a forced-landing area. If by flying at an angle to the wind, you can keep a forced landing area in reach, then do so. If at all possible, make a normal approach. A steeper approach will be required, if there are high obstacles.

Now, in the low reconnaissance, verify what was seen in the high reconnaissance. Pick up anything that you could have missed earlier. Check especially for wires, slopes and small crevices, because these are particularly difficult to see from a higher altitude.

A low reconnaissance begins just after your approach entry into the confined area. It ends at touchdown. During the interim, objects on the ground can be better identified and the height of obstacles better estimated. The view of the approach path is greatly improved. The approach should be as close to normal as possible. If new information warrants a change in flight path or angle of descent, it should be made. However, if a major change in angle of descent is required, make a go-around. If a go-around decision is made, it should be done prior to losing effective translational lift.

Once the commitment is made to land, the approach will be terminated in a hover at an altitude that will conserve the ground effect. Check the landing spot carefully before actually landing. Maintain rotor operating rpm until the stability of the helicopter on the terrain can be checked for a secure and safe position. In many cases, not doing so could mean a long walk out.

Before taking off from a confined area, make a walking ground reconnaissance to determine the point from which it should be initiated. This is to ensure a maximum amount of available area, and how best to get the helicopter from the landing spot to a position from which the takeoff is proposed.

First thing, check the wind. If the rotor was left turning after landing, walk a sufficient distance from the craft to ensure that the downwash of the blades doesn't interfere. Light dust or grass may be dropped and the direction they are blown observed.

Next, go to the downwind end of the area and mark a position for takeoff, so that the tail and main rotors will have sufficient clearance from obstructions. A sturdy marker, such as a heavy stone or log, should be used as this marker.

If rearward flight is required to reach the takeoff position, reference markers should be placed in front of the helicopter in such a way that a ground track can be safely followed to the takeoff position. If wind conditions and available area permit, hover-taxi downwind from the landing position to the takeoff spot.

In preparing for the actual takeoff from a confined area, first visualize the angle over obstacles from the takeoff position. The flight path should be over the lowest barrier that allows for taking best advantage of wind and terrain. Make the takeoff and climb as near normal as possible. Again, it's better to clear the obstructions by a few feet at normal rotor rpm than to sacrifice rotor rpm by attempting to clear by a large margin. Wind conditions should seriously be considered during the takeoff.

In general, flying over good terrain is preferable to heading directly into the wind, depending, of course, on the speed of the wind and the relative height of obstacles.

Because of its unique flight characteristics, a helicopter is capable of many missions to other aircraft can perform. You must, however, realize the hazards involved and know also what precautions to take in preserving the craft, as well as your life.

Here are a few basic and general precautionary rules that should consider and keep in mind:

- [ ] Don't perform acrobatic maneuvers.
- [ ] Don't check magnetos in flight in lieu of ground checks during runup.
- [ ] Use caution when adjusting mixture in flight.
- [ ] Always taxi (air) slowly (about as fast as you can walk).
- [ ] Always check balance prior to flying.
- [ ] Use caution when hovering on the leeward side of buidings or obstruction.
- [ ] Don't hover at an altitude that will place you in the shaded area of the height-velocity chart.
- [ ] Always hover for a moment before beginning a new flight.
- [ ] When practicing hovering turns, sideward flight and similar low airspeed maneuvers, be especially careful to maintain proper rpm.
- [ ] When flying in rough, gusty air, use special care to maintain proper rpm.
- [ ] Always clear the area overhead, ahead, to each side and below before entering practice autorotations.
- [ ] Make sure any object placed in the cockpit of your helicopter is secured to prevent fouling of controls or mechanisms.
- [ ] Except in sideward or rearward flight, always fly the aircraft from references ahead.

Rotor RPM Operating Limits

Limits of rotor rpm vary with each type of craft. In general, the lower limit is determined primarily by the control characteristics of a particular helicopter during autorotation. Since the tail rotor is driven by the main rotor, a minimum main rotor rpm exists at which tail rotor thrust is sufficient for proper heading control. Below this minimum main-rotor rpm, full rudder travel will not maintain heading under certain conditions of flight.

The upper limit for rotor rpm is based on both autorotative characteristics and structural strength of the rotor system. Structural tests, plus an adequate margin for safety, are required by FAA safety standards for the certification of the aircraft.

Extreme Attitudes and Overcontrolling

Avoid all maneuvers which would place the craft in danger of extreme and unusual attitudes. Design characteristics of a helicopter preclude the possibility of safe inverted flight.

Avoid helicopter loading that will cause an extreme tail-low attitude when taking off to a hover. Aft center CG is dangerous while hovering, and even more so in flight because of limited forward cyclic travel.

Avoid heavy loading forward of the CG. The result is limited aft cyclic travel, endangering controllability.

Avoid an extreme nose-low attitude when executing a normal takeoff. Such an attitude may require more power than the engine can deliver, and it will also allow the helicopter to settle to the ground in an unsafe landing attitude. In the event of a forced landing, only a comparatively level attitude can assure a safe touchdown.

Avoid abrupt applications of rearward cyclic. The violent backward-pitching action of the rotor disc may cause the main rotor to flex downward into the tailboom.

Avoid large or unnecessary movements of the cyclic while in a hover. Such movements of the cyclic can, under certain conditions, cause sufficient loss of lift to make the craft settle to the ground.

Flight Technique in Hot Weather

As discussed in an earlier chapter, hot temperatures drive density altitude up. When you encounter hot weather, piloting skills call for special techniques. Follow these rules religiously:

- ☐ Make full use of wind and translational lift.
- ☐ Hover as low as possible and no longer than absolutely necessary.
- ☐ Maintain maximum allowable engine rpm.
- ☐ Accelerate very slowly into forward flight.
- ☐ Employ running takeoffs and landings, whenever possible.
- ☐ Use caution in maximum performance takeoffs and landings from steep approaches.
- ☐ Avoid high rates of descent in all approaches.

High Altitude Pilot Technique

Of the three major factors limiting helicopter performance at high altitudes (gross weight, density altitude, and wind), only gross weight may be controlled by the pilot of an unsupercharged helicopter. At the expense of range, you may carry smaller amounts of fuel to improve performance, increase the number of passengers or the amount of baggage. Where practical, use running landings and takeoffs. Make maximum use of favorable winds, with landings and takeoffs directly into them when possible. Other factors sometimes dictate otherwise.

When the wind blows over large obstructions, such as mountain ridges, turbulent conditions are set up. The wind blowing up the slope on the windward side is usually relatively smooth. However, on the leeward side, the wind spills rapidly down the slope, similar to the way water flows down a rough steambed. This tumbling action sets up strong downdrafts and causes very turbulent air. These violent downdrafts can cause aircraft to strike the sides of mountains. Therefore, when approaching mountain ridges against the wind, make an extra altitude allowance to assure safe terrain clearance. Where pronounced mountain ridges and strong winds are present, a clearance of 2000 to 3000 feet AGL is considered a desirable minimum. Also, it's advisable to climb to the crossing altitude well before reaching the mountain barrier to avoid having to make the climb in a persistent downdraft (Fig. 13-3).

When operating over mountainous terrain, fly on the upwind side of ridges. The safest approach is usually made lengthwise of the ridge at about a 45-degree angle. Fly near the upwind edge to avoid possible downdrafts and to be in position to autorotate down the upwind side of the slope in case of forced landing. Riding the updraft in this manner results in a lower rate of descent, improved glide ratio, and a greater choice of a landing areas.

Tall Grass and Water Operations

Tall grass will tend to disperse or absorb the ground cushion that you're used to over firm ground. More power will be required to hover, and takeoff could be tricky. Before attempting to hover over tall grass, make sure that at least two to three inches more manifold pressure are available than is required to hover over normal terrain.

Operations over water with a smooth or glassy surface makes altitude determination difficult. Exercise caution to prevent the helicopter from inadvertently striking the water. This problem doesn't exist over rough water, but a very rough water surface could disperse the ground effect and thereby require more power to hover. Movements of the water surface, wind ripples, waves, current flow, or even agitation by the chopper's own rotor wash will tend to give you a false sense of aircraft movement (Fig. 13-4).

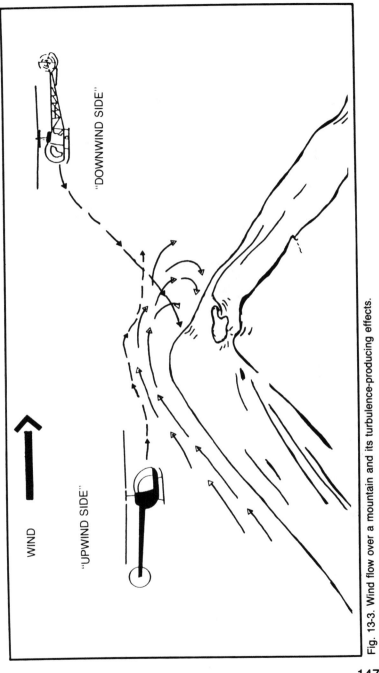

WIND

"UPWIND SIDE"

"DOWNWIND SIDE"

Fig. 13-3. Wind flow over a mountain and its turbulence-producing effects.

Fig. 13-4. Water operations require extreme care because of difficulty in judging altitude while hovering over a reflective surface. Ripples in water will give pilot a false sense of movement.

Carburetor Icing

Carburetor icing is a frequent cause of engine failure. The vaporization of fuel, combined with the expansion of air as it passes through the carburetor, causes a sudden cooling of the mixture. The temperature of the air passing through the carburetor can drop as much as 60 degrees F within a fraction of a second. Water vapor in the air is squeezed out by this cooling, and if the temperature in the carburetor reaches 32 degrees F or below, the moisture will be deposited as frost or ice inside the carburetor passages. Even a slight accumulation of such deposits reduces power and can lead to a complete engine failure, particularly when the throttle is partially or fully closed.

On dry days or when the temp is well below freezing, moisture in the air isn't generally enough to cause much trouble. But, if the temperature is 20 to 70 degrees F, with visible moisture or high humidity, the pilot should be constantly on the alert for carb ice. During low or closed throttle settings, an engine is particularly susceptible to carburetor icing.

Indications of carb ice include unexplained loss of rpm or manifold pressure; the carburetor air temp indicating in the "red" (danger) arc or "yellow" arc; and engine roughness. A loss of manifold pressure will generally give the first indication. However, due to the many small control changes (settings) made in the throttle and collective, this might be less noticeable. So, a close check of the carb air temperature gauge is necessary so that carburetor heat may be adjusted to keep the carb air temp gauge out of the red and yellow arcs.

Carburetor air temperature gauges are marked with a green arc, representing the range of desired operating temps; a yellow arc represents the range of temperatures in which caution should be exercised, since icing is possible; and a red arc represents the maximum operating temperature limit, or is used to represent the most dangerous range in which carb ice can be anticipated. The carb heat control should be adjusted so that the carburetor air temperature remains in the green arc.

The carburetor heater is an anti-icing device that preheats air before it reaches the carburetor. This preheating can be used to melt ice or snow entering the intake duct; melt ice that forms in the carburetor passages (provided the accumulation isn't too great); and to keep the fuel mixture above the freezing point, preventing formation of carb ice.

When conditions are favorable for carb ice, you should make the proper check for its presence often. Check the manifold pressure gauge reading, then apply full carburetor heat and leave it on until you're certain that if ice was present, it has been removed. (During this check, a constant throttle and collective setting should be maintained.) Carb heat should then be returned to the "off" position (cold). If the manifold pressure gauge indicates higher than when the check was started, and carb air temp gauges indicates a safe operation range, crab ice has been removed.

Fuel injection systems have replaced carburetors in some craft. In the fuel injection system, the fuel is normally injected into the system either directly ahead of the intake valves or into the cylinders themselves. In the carburetor system, the fuel enters the airstream at the throttle valve. The fuel injection system is generally considered to be less susceptible to icing than the carb system.

Effect of Altitude on Instrument Readings

The thinner air of higher altitudes causes the airspeed indicator to read slow in relation to True Airspeed. True airspeed may be roughly computed by adding to the Indicated Airspeed two percent of the indicated airspeed for each 1000 feet of altitude MSL. For example, an indicated speed of 80 mph at 5000 feet MSL will be a True airspeed of about 88 mph. This computation may be made more accurately with the use of a computer.

Manifold pressure is reduced approximately one inch per 1000 feet above sea level. If you have 28 inches manifold pressure at 1000 feet, only 22 inches manifold pressure must be considered when planning flights to higher altitudes.

14

Introduction to the Helicopter Flight Manual

It's your responsibility as pilot in command (PIC) to know all pertinent information for each helicopter you fly. The helicopter flight manual is designed to provide you with a general knowledge of the particular helicopter and the information necessary for its safe and efficient operation. Its function isn't to teach you to fly, but rather to provide you with the best possible operating instructions, under most circumstances. The manual isn't intended as a substitute for sound judgment, however, as emergencies and other unforeseen situations may require modification of these procedures.

A helicopter flight manual accompanies each certificated helicopter. Although the manual for a particular craft may contain information identical to that contained in the flight manual for other helicopters of the same make and model, it may also contain data which is peculiar only to that one helicopter, especially the information on weight and balance. Helicopter flight manuals are prepared and furnished by the aircraft's manufacturers. Much of the information contained in them is required by FARs, Part 27, "Airworthiness Standards: Normal Category Rotorcraft." However, manufacturers often include additional information that is helpful to the pilot but which isn't specifically required.

When the helicopter manual contains information required by regulations that doesn't appear as placards in the craft, the manual must be carried in the machine at all times. The statement, "This document must be carried in the aircraft at all times," will appear somewhere on the manual if such conditions exist.

Most flight manuals would include the following, under chapters, sections, headings or a similar breakdown in information:

- ☐ General Information.
- ☐ Limitations.
- ☐ Normal Procedures.
- ☐ Emergency and Malfunction Procedures.
- ☐ Performance Data.
- ☐ Weight & Balance.
- ☐ Aircraft Handling, Servicing and Maintenance.

General Information

Data presented here would include an introduction, if there is one, method of presentation, helicopter description, certification, design and construction, and general dimensional data.

The Introduction might read something to the effect: "The pilot's flight manual has been prepared with but one very fundamental goal in mind; that is, to provide the pilot with all information necessary to accomplish the intended mission with the maximum amount of safety and economy possible . . ."

The method of presentation means just that: Information in various sections is presented in different formats. It can be presented as a narrative, charts, tabular form, etc., or a combination. In any case, it will be described here. Notes, step-by-step procedures are also explained, such as the following examples:

The "Caution" symbol is used to alert you that damage to equipment could result, if the procedure step isn't following exactly.

The "Warning" symbol is used here to bring to your attention that not only damage to equipment but personal injury could occur, if the instruction is disregarded.

The Helicopter Description gives an overall description of the craft. It may describe it as fast, lightweight, turbine-powered, all-purpose, etc. It would also give other key tidbits, such as its different uses and configurations: ambulance, internal/external cargo capability, aerial survey, patrol, photographic, air/sea rescue, agricultural, forestry and police applications, to name a few.

"Design and Construction" gives details as to material makeup, crew and passenger seating, powerplant, and some of the craft's outstanding features, among others.

As an example, one entry in the Hughes 500D (Model 369D) explains: ". . . is a turbine powered, rotary-wing aircraft constructed primarily of aluminum alloy. The main rotor is five-bladed and fully articulated, the tail rotor is a two-bladed, antitorque semi-rigid type. Power from the turboshaft engine is coupled to the main and rail rotors by draft shafts and two transmissions. An overrunning (one-way) clutch in the drive between the engine and main transmission permits freewheeling of the rotors for autorotational descent."

"General Dimensional Data" would include rotor characteristics, rotor speeds, control rigging of the main and tail rotor. Often general information graphs and charts are included for such conversions dealing with velocity, temperature, liquid, linear, weight, and pressure. Also, a three-view drawing of the particular craft showing its principal dimensions may be included (Fig. 14-1).

Limitations

All aircraft have certain parameters within which they must fly. With the helicopter, these limitations would include airspeed limits, rotor speed, weight and balance, powerplant, and others. In some instances, limitations are as easy to comply with as keeping a needle within a green or yellow arc, while others, such as weight and balance, will take more thought and preplanning.

The section would include all important operating limitations that must be observed during normal operations. Airspeed Limits must be shown on the airspeed indicator (ASI) by a color coding or must be displayed in the form of a placard. A red radial line must be placed on the ASI to show the airspeed limit beyond which operation is dangerous. This speed is also known as the "never-exceed" speed or V_{ne}. A yellow arc is used to indicate cautionary operating ranges, and of course, a green arc for safe or normal operation. Required information on Rotor Limits are marked on the tachometer by red radial lines and yellow arcs respectively, with normal operating ranges marked with a green arc, much as speed markings. Information for rotor limits, as well as airspeed, is sometimes given in the form of a chart or graph.

Powerplant limitation information will explain all powerplant limits and the required markings on the powerplant instruments.

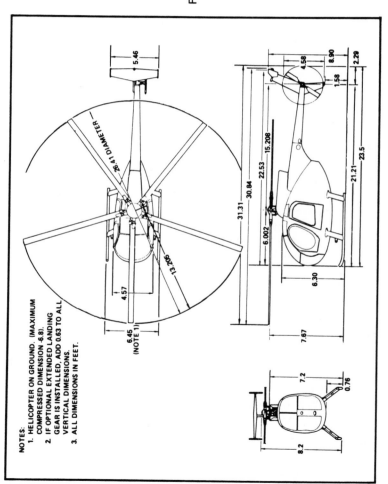

Fig. 14-1. Hughes 500D dimensions.

NOTES:
1. HELICOPTER ON GROUND. (MAXIMUM COMPRESSED DIMENSION -6.8).
2. IF OPTIONAL EXTENDED LANDING GEAR IS INSTALLED, ADD 0.63 TO ALL VERTICAL DIMENSIONS.
3. ALL DIMENSIONS IN FEET.

This will include such items as fuel octane rating, idling rpm, manifold pressure, oil pressure, oil temperature, cylinder-head temp, fuel pressure, mixture, and others.

Normal Procedures

This section of the manual contains information concerning normal procedures for takeoff and landing, appropriate airspeeds peculiar to the rotorcraft's operating characteristics and other pertinent information necessary for safe operations. This portion may include the following procedures: checklists for preflight, before starting engine, starting engine, warmup, takeoff, inflight procedures, and landing.

Normal procedures would also include such operations as low-speed maneuvering, practice autorotations, doors-off flight, and post-flight. Depending on the machine, of course, it could give you an instrument panel rundown, explain pilot controls and even give you a rundown on the fuel system (Fig. 14-2).

Engine Start Procedures:

1. Mixture, IDLE CUT-OFF.
2. Fuel valve, ON.
3. Throttle friction releases, throttle closed.
4. Fuel boost, ON; check pressure.
5. Mixture FULL-RICH, 2.5-3.0 seconds; return to IDLE CUT-OFF.
6. Fuel boost, OFF.
7. Ignition switch, BOTH.
8. Engage starter.
9. When engine starts, mixture FULL-RICH.
10. Heater fan (exhaust muff heater), ON.
11. Set engine rpm at approximately 1400.
12. Fuel boost, ON.
13. Check engine oil pressure 25 psi minimum.
14. Alternator switch, ON.

Emergency and Malfunction Procedures

These procedures may warrant a section of their own, or they could be combined with "Normal Operating Procedures." However, in either case, they should be studied until they become second nature to you, and marked off for quick reference.

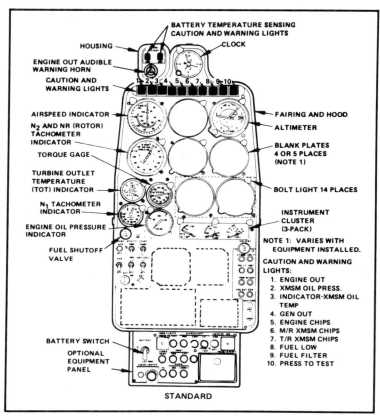

Fig. 14-2. A typical instrument panel for a light turbine helicopter.

This section should cover such items as engine failure, ditching, tail rotor failure, and how to recognize and correct such emergencies. It would also contain failure of specialized, optional equipment, such as cyclic trim or the power turbine governor.

Recommendations for correcting such situations may read like this example on engine failure:

1. Establish a 60 mph autorotation.
2. If less than 2000 feet AGL, pick a landing spot, and proceed with autorotation landing.
3. Pull mixture control to IDLE CUT-OFF, when time permits, to stop flow of fuel from nozzles.
4. If altitude permits (cyclic can be gripped between knees to achieve the following):

a. With mixture in IDLE CUT-OFF.

b. Throttle—crack about 1/2 inch.

c. Starter—press to engage.

d. Mixture—push to FULL RICH position when engine fires.

(Note: If fuel boost pump was on at time of engine stoppage, a flooded condition could have resulted, necessitating additional use of the starter.)

Performance Data

It's primarily from the information taken from graphs and charts found in this section that you're able to plot and figure how the craft will operate. This section should include such information as: rates of climb and hovering ceilings, together with the corresponding airspeeds and other pertinent information, including the calculated effect of altitude and temperature, maximum allowable wind for safe operation near the ground, and sufficient other data to outline the limiting heights and corresponding speeds for safe landing after power failure.

Using the Density Altitude and Best Rate of Climb Speed charts, find the best rate of climb speed you should use when at a pressure altitude of 7000 feet with a temperature of 20 degrees C (Fig. 14-3).

1. Locate 20 degrees C along the bottom of the DA chart. Follow its line vertically, until it intersects 7000 feet pressure altitude. Move horizontally left to read a density altitude of approximately 9000 feet.

2. Using the Best Rate of Climb chart (Fig. 14-4) locate 9000 feet DA on the left side. Move horizontally from this point until intersecting the dark vertical line. From this point drop vertically straight down the graph to the craft's best rate of climb speed of 59 to 60 knots.

"Maximum allowable wind" for safe operations near the ground will be noted by a statement in most flight manuals, similar to the following: "When hovering with wind from the left, expect random yaw oscillations; with wind from right, expect random pitch and roll oscillations in winds 10 knots and above."

Limiting heights and corresponding speeds for safe landing after power failure are generally incorporated in a chart called the "Airspeed vs. Altitude Limitations Chart" or "Height-Velocity Curve, Diagram or Chart." This chart generally appears in the performance section of the manual, but occasionally can be found in the "Operating Limitations Section."

You'll notice in the Height-Velocity Chart presented in Fig. 14-5, the recommended takeoff profile. A normal takeoff would be to liftoff to about 8 feet AGL and accelerate to around 36 knots before initiating a climb. Once the climb is started, it recommends

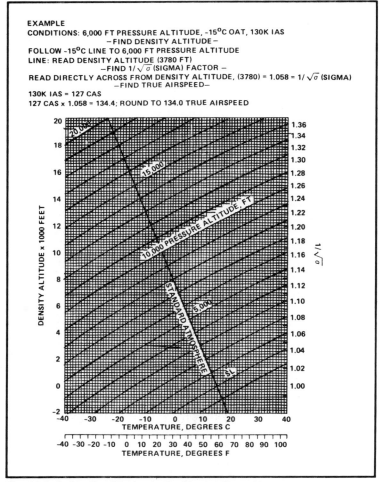

Fig. 14-3. A density altitude chart with sample problem.

a gradual increase in airspeed to 60 knots as a height of 75 feet AGL is attained.

Care should be taken to avoid operations within the shaded area of the Height-Velocity Chart, as it signifies an unsafe operation.

All helicopters will normally have at least one placard displayed in a conspicuous position that has a direct and important bearing on safe operation of that particular helicopter. These placards will

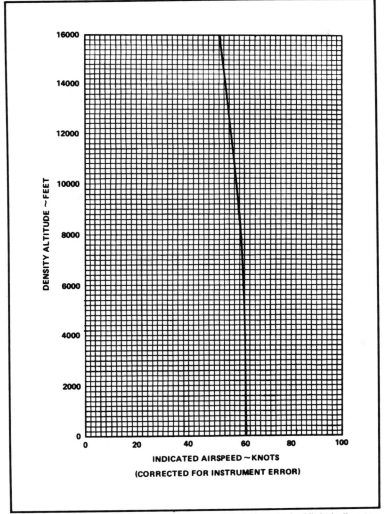

Fig. 14-4. Best rate of climb airspeed versus altitude for a typical light helicopter.

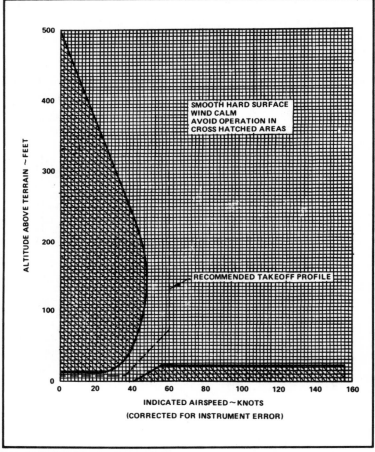

Fig. 14-5. Height-velocity envelope.

generally appear also in the machine's flight manual in the "Operating Limitations" section under the heading of "Placards, Caution or Warning." An example of this might be, "Strobe anticollision lights should be turned OFF during prolonged hover or ground operation over concrete, to avoid possible pilot distraction." Another example might be, "Solo pilot operation from the LEFT seat only."

Weight and Balance

The Weight and Balance portion must include rotorcraft

weights and center of gravity (CG) limits, together with the items of equipment on which the empty weight is based. This will generally require the use of a chart or graph from which you can compute the CG position for any given loading situation (Fig. 14-6, 14-7).

If the unusable fuel supply in any tank exceeds one gallon or five percent of the tank capacity, whichever is greater, a warning shall be provided to indicate to flight personnel that when the quantity indicator reads "zero" the remaining fuel in the tank can't be used for flight. A complete explanation and sample problem on weight and balance follows in the next chapter.

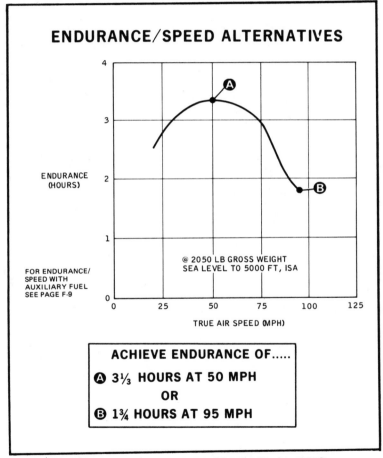

Fig. 14-6. Endurance versus true airspeed for the Hughes 300C.

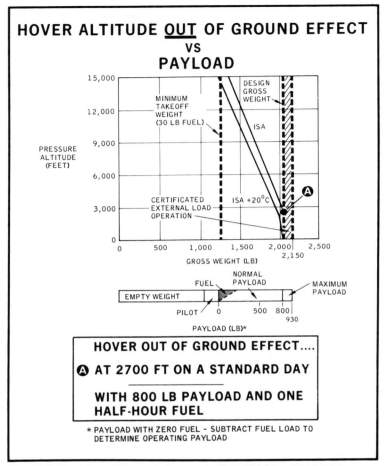

Fig. 14-7. Hovering ceiling out of ground effect (HOGE ceiling) versus payload for the Hughes 300C.

15

Weight and Balance

All helicopters, like all aircraft, are designed for certain weight and balance conditions. But it's you, the PIC, who is responsible for making sure that the specified weight and balance limitations are met before takeoff. Any pilot who does takeoff in a helicopter that isn't within the designed weight and balance condition is not only violating FAA regulations but is inviting disaster.

Four kinds of weight must be considered in the loading of every machine. They are empty weight, useful load, gross weight and maximum (allowable) gross weight.

Empty weight can be described as the weight of the helicopter, including the structure, the powerplant, all fixed equipment, all fixed ballast, unusable fuel, undrainable oil, and the total quantity of both engine coolant and hydraulic fluid.

Useful load is the weight of the pilot, passengers, baggage (including removable ballast) usable fuel and drainable oil.

Gross weight is simply the empty weight plus the useful load. The sum of these two weights must now be compared with the fourth weight to be considered—maximum gross weight.

Maximum gross weight is the heaviest weight for which the craft is certificated to fly or operate under varying conditions. Some helicopter manufacturers use the term *basic weight* in determining the weight and balance of their helicopters. Basic weight includes the empty weight, as previously defined, plus the weight of the drainable oil. Whenever the term "basic weight" is used, it should be understood that this is its meaning.

Although a helicopter is certificated for a specified maximum gross weight, it will not be safe to take off with this load under all situations. Conditions that affect takeoff, climb, hovering, and landing performance may require the off-loading of fuel, passengers, or baggage to a weight less than the maximum allowable. Such conditions would include high altitudes, high temperatures, and high humidity, the combination of which makes for a high density altitude. Additional factors to consider are takeoff and landing surfaces, takeoff and landing distances, and the presence of obstacles.

Because of the various adverse conditions that may exist, many times you'll have to decide the needs of the type of mission to be flown and load your craft accordingly. For example, if all seats are occupied and maximum baggage is carried, gross weight limitations could dictate that less than max fuel be carried. On the other hand, if you're interested in range, you may elect to carry a full load but fewer passengers and less baggage.

Balance

Not only must you consider the gross weight of the helicopter, but you must also determine that the load is arranged to fall within the allowable center of gravity (CG) range, which is specified in the helicopter flight manual. The CG is the point where the copter is in balance—the point at which all the weight of the system is considered to be concentrated. If the helicopter were suspended by a string attached to the *CG point*, the craft's fuselage would remain parallel to the ground, much as a perfectly balanced teeter-totter. The allowable range in which the CG must fall is referred to as the *CG range*. The exact location and length of this range is specified for each machine, but it usually extends a short distance fore and aft of the main rotor mast. For most helicopter types, the location of the CG must be kept within much narrower limits than for airplanes—in some cases less than three inches.

The ideal condition is to have a machine in such perfect balance that the fuselage will remain horizontal in hovering flight, with no cyclic pitch control necessary except that necessary for windage. The fuselage acts as a pendulum suspended from the rotor.

Any change in the CG changes the angle at which it hangs from this point of support. If the weight is concentrated directly under the rotor mast, the helicopter hangs horizontal; if the center-of-gravity is too far aft of the mast, the machine hangs with nose tilted up; and if the CG is too far forward of the mast, the nose tilts down (Fig. 15-1). Hence, out-of-balance loading of the chopper makes control more difficult and decreases maneuverability, since cyclic travel is restricted in the direction opposite of the CG location. Because helicopters are relatively narrow and high sideward speeds will not be attained, lateral balance presents no problems in normal flight instruction and passenger flights, but some light helicopters specify the seat from which solo flight must be made. However, if external loads are carried in such a position that a large, lateral displacement of the cyclic is required to maintain level flight, fore and aft cyclic movements might be limited.

CG Forward of Allowable Limits

This condition arises more often in two-place helicopters—a heavy pilot and passenger take off without baggage or proper ballast located aft of the rotor mast. The condition will become worse as the flight progresses, due to fuel consumption, if the main fuel tank is located behind the rotor mast.

You'll recognize this condition after coming to a hover following a vertical takeoff. The copter will have a nose-low attitude, and an excessive rearward cyclic will be required to hold a hover in a no-wind condition—if hovering flight can be maintained at all. Flight under this condition shouldn't be continued, since the possibility of running out of rearward cyclic control will increase rapidly

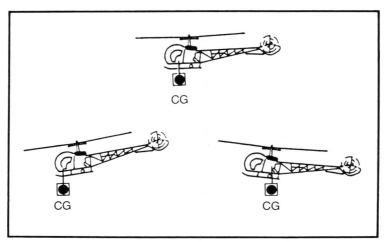

Fig. 15-1. How CG affects helicopter pitch attitude.

as fuel is consumed. You might even find it impossible to increase the pitch attitude sufficiently to bring the chopper to a stop. Also, in case of engine failure and the resulting autorotation, sufficient cyclic might not be available to flare properly for the landing.

Hovering in a strong wind will make a forward CG less easy to recognize, since less rearward displacement of the cyclic will be required than when hovering in a no-wind condition. You should therefore consider the wind speed in which you're hovering and its relation to the rearward displacement of the cyclic in determining if a critical balance condition exists.

CG Aft of Maximum Limits

Without proper ballast in the cockpit, this condition could arise when: a lightweight pilot takes off solo with a full load of fuel located aft of the rotor mast; a lightweight pilot takes off with maximum baggage allowed in a compartment located behind the rotor mast; or a lightweight pilot takes off with a combination of baggage and substantial fuel where both are aft of the rotor mast. You'll recognize this condition after bringing the craft to a hover, following a vertical takeoff. The chopper will have a tail-low attitude, and an excessive forward cyclic will be required to hold a hover in a no-wind condition, if a hover can be maintained at all. If there's a wind, an even greater forward displacement will be required.

If you continue flight in this condition, you could find it impossible to fly at high airspeeds due to insufficient forward cyclic displacement to hold a nose-low attitude. This particular condition could become quite dangerous if gusty or rough air accelerates the machine to a higher airspeed than forward cyclic will allow. The nose will start to rise and full forward cyclic might be insufficient to hold it down or lower it once it does rise.

Weight and Balance Information

When a helicopter is delivered from the factory, the empty weight, empty weight CG, and useful load for each particular craft are noted on a weight and balance data sheet included in the helicopter flight manual. These quantities will vary for different helicopters of a given series, depending on variations in fixed equipment included in each helicopter when delivered (Figs. 15-2, 15-3).

If, after delivery, additional fixed equipment is added, or if some is removed, or a major repair or alteration is made which may affect the empty weight, empty weight CG or useful load, the weight

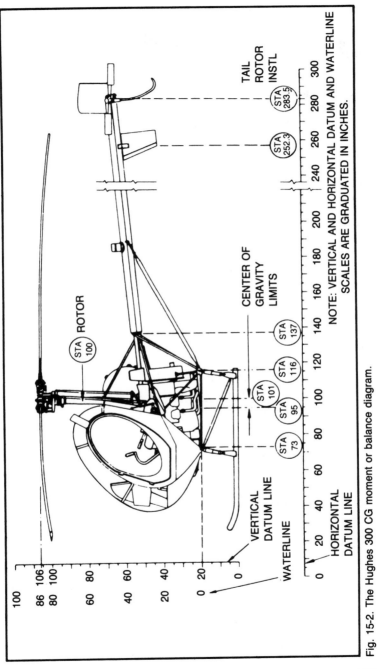

Fig. 15-2. The Hughes 300 CG moment or balance diagram.

167

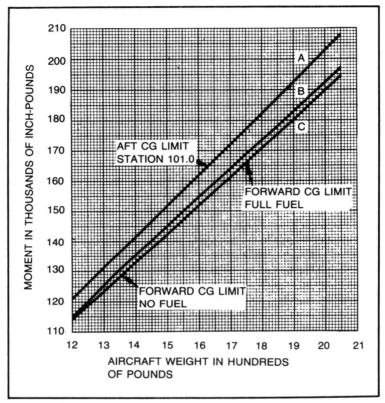

Fig. 15-3. Loading chart.

and balance data must be revised to reflect this new information and its effect on that particular craft. All weight and balance changes will be entered in the appropriate aircraft records. This generally will be the aircraft logbook. Make sure you use the latest weight and balance data in computing all loading problems.

Sample Weight and Balance Problem

In loading a helicopter for flight you have to answer two very basic questions: Is its gross weight within the maximum allowable gross weight, and does that weight's CG fall within the allowable CG range?

To answer the first question, merely add the weight of the items comprising the useful load (pilot, passengers, usable fuel, drainable oil and baggage) to the empty weight of the machine. Then check the total weight obtained to see that it doesn't exceed maximum allowable gross weight. If basic weight is used in computing weight and balance, then the weight of the oil is included with this weight.

To answer the second question, use the loading chart or loading table in the aircraft's flight manual for the particular helicopter being flown.

Sample Problem: Determine if the gross weight and CG are within allowable limits under the following conditions based on the sample loading charts.

Pounds

Basic Weight.....................................	1070
Fuel (full tank—30 gallons)........................	180
Pilot (Station 83.2)................................	170
Passenger (right hand—Station 83.2)................	170
Passenger (center—Station 80.0)...................	170

By adding the individual weights together, you should come out with a gross weight sum of 1760 pounds. Now, does the gross weight fall at or below the maximum allowable gross weight specified for this helicopter? With a maximum gross of 2050 pounds, 1760 gross is well below max.

How about CG range; does the CG point fall within the CG range? With the use of the "Load Weight—Pounds" chart, find the moment in thousands of inch-pounds for each position or station. With the sample, as stated above, it should look something like this:

	Pounds	**Moment**
Basic Weight...........................	1070	108,915
Fuel (full tank—30 gallons).................	180	19,260
Pilot (Station 83.2).......................	170	14,144
Passenger (right hand—Station 83.2)........	170	14,144
Passenger (center—Station 80.0)...........	170	13,600
	1760	170,063

Where will the total moment and weight fall within the CG range? To find out, simply go to the loading chart and plot the CG. First, plot the aircraft's gross weight in hundreds of pounds across the bottom of the chart, and the total moment in thousands of inch-pounds vertically on the left side. Once these two points have been found, it's simply a matter of drawing a line vertically up the chart from pounds and a line horizontally across the chart from the moment. Where these two intersect on the chart will be your craft's CG point. Does this CG point fall within the CG range (the bold, black lines)? Sure it does. It's between lines 'A' and 'B' and, therefore, your loading meets all balance requirements.

Sample problems such as this should be worked until you feel comfortable using the craft's charts and graphs. It also makes you more familiar with the operation of your particular helicopter, and this means a safer operation.

16
Maintenance

With helicopters, more so than with small airplanes, maintenance is a continuous, ongoing process. In addition to annual and/or 100-hour inspection requirements (which most aircraft have anyway), and the usual major-component TBO (time between overhauls) schedules, helicopters very often have 50-hour, 25-hour, 10-hour, and even hourly or daily inspection and service requirements—some mandated by the manufacturer, others mandated by FAA Airworthiness Directives. Moreover, when a life-limited part reaches its TBO, or when a service part turns up defective during inspection, the helicopter must be grounded; it cannot be flown again until the defective component(s) are replaced. This is in contrast to the situation that often prevails with fixed-wing aircraft, in which minor defects are often allowed to accumulate between inspection periods, or where numerous flights may be knowingly made with nonessential equipment inoperative. On a helicopter, there is little equipment that can truly be considered nonessential. Hence, the helicopter's maintenance needs are much more pressing (Fig. 16-1).

Helicopter maintenance also tends to be expensive, as anyone who has more than a passing familiarity with rotor-wing aircraft knows. A single rotor blade can cost $10,000 or more; a transmission overhaul (needed every 1,200 hours on some ships) can run $8,000. Even such otherwise mundane items as control-system rod ends (the kind with spherical bearings) can cost upwards of $100

Fig. 16-1. Helicopters have fixed component TBO or retirement schedules and strict 100-hour (and often 50-hour, 25-hour, or even hourly) inspection requirements which must be adhered to if the ship is to remain legal—and safe.

apiece. Spark plugs currently list for $16 each, in the copper-core versions; but most operators prefer platinum or iridium-tipped spark plugs, costing $24 to $44 each.

There are many reasons why helicopters are so maintenance-intensive. One is the complexity of mechanical systems. (One look at the rotor head of a large helicopter such as a Sikorsky S-61 will tell you a lot about why helicopters cost as much as they do.) The transmission, control system, tail rotor, and rotor hub of a fully articulated helicopter have a high parts count, and the parts are in many cases of extremely intricate design, manufactured of exotic materials, often to unimaginably close tolerances. Yet all of the moving parts in a helicopter (and many that aren't moving) are subjected to repeated stress cycles in normal operation. Moreover, vibrations felt by one part are often propagated to other parts downstream. Engineers take these factors into consideration in determining an estimated service life for each critical component on the helicopter, and the most critical components (such as rotor blades, rotor bearings, etc.) are subjected to long-term laboratory fatigue testing to determine ultimate fatigue life under dynamic load conditions. Component TBOs are then set allowing comfortable margins between TBO and ultimate fatigue life. In the case of components that are not assigned a TBO, inspection intervals (100 hours, 50 hours, or whatever) are set and the component gets service on an IRAN (inspect and replace as necessary) basis.

The pilot's role in performing required maintenance on a helicopter is a relatively small one. Under Part 91 of the Federal Aviation Regulations, the pilot is responsible for the airworthy condition of the helicopter, and the pilot (*not* the mechanic) is responsible for seeing that required inspections are done and Airworthiness Directives complied with. Under FAR Part 43, however, pilots are not actually allowed to perform repairs or alterations themselves (unless the pilot also is a properly certificated Airframe and Powerplant mechanic); instead, pilots are allowed to perform only preventive maintenance. According to FAR Part 1, *preventive maintenance* "means simple or minor preservation operations and the replacement of small standard parts not involving complex assembly operations." Appendix A of FAR Part 43 gives a further, detailed listing of items that the FAA specifically considers to be "preventive maintenance" (performable by pilots). Included are such items as changing oil, cleaning fuel and oil stainers, replacing batteries, cleaning and gapping spark plugs, repairing upholstery, replenishing hydraulic fluid, applying preservative coatings to parts, replacing side windows, servicing struts, replacing defective safety wire or cotter pins, replacing landing light bulbs and reflectors, repainting non-balanced control surfaces and exterior items, and miscellaneous lubrication.

Many of the aforementioned preventive maintenance items—battery replacement and spark plug cleaning, for example—involve procedures that are no different for helicopters than for fixed-wing aircraft. We will touch on some of these areas further below; however, space limitations preclude a detailed recapitulation of all preventive maintenance procedures here. Interested readers are encouraged to consult *Lightplane Owner's Maintenance Guide*, TAB book 2244.

Many of a helicopter's maintenance needs are unique, and the knowledgeable pilot is in a good position to spot and diagnose trouble signs well in advance of taking the ship to a mechanic. (Also, the knowledgeable pilot is in an excellent position to forestall costly maintenance problems by applying good operating practices.) No helicopter operator should consider his or her education as a pilot complete until having gotten a firm grounding in the unique maintenance requirements of helicopters, particularly the type of model of helicopter that the pilot flies (Fig. 16-2). Obviously, only general guidelines can be given here, although where possible we will make specific reference to the Robinson R-22, Enstrom F-28A, and Hughes 269B.

Ground Handling

Extreme care must be used in ground handling any helicopter. Indiscriminate pushing or pulling on various parts of a small helicopter can easily cause damage. Always read and follow the advice given in the Maintenance section of the helicopter's operating handbook, or seek the advice of a knowledgeable pilot or mechanic before attempting to maneuver a helicopter on the ground.

Most small helicopters such as the R-22, Enstrom, or Hughes 300 are maneuvered on the ground using ground handling wheels. In some cases, the wheels are designed to be stowed and carried in flight. To deploy the wheels, it is usually necessary to pull a safety pin, rotate a lever 180 degrees (past center), and reinstall the safety pin to keep the wheel in the down position. With the Hughes 300, the tail boom must be lowered first by applying hand force directly in front of the tail rotor gearbox until the tail skid touches the ground. *The gear-deployment handle has a tendency to "snap over" with the weight of the ship of the wheel.* Use caution to see that hands, feet, etc. are never in the way of the gear handle as the wheels are being locked in place; serious injuries have resulted when gear handles have unexpectedly let go.

To move the R-22 or Hughes 300 on wheels, the pilot must steady the tail boom (at the tail rotor gearbox) so as to balance the weight of the ship on the tires. Then the ship can be maneuvered carefully, with extra persons applying force *in specified areas only*. With the R-22, extra pushing may be done at any of the vertical steel truss tubes located aft of the engine. Alternatively, someone may gently push on the nose of the ship. The helicopter should *not* be moved by gripping vertical fins, horizontal stabilizer structure, tail rotor, or control rods. *Apply pressure only in approved areas*.

If it should become necessary to rotate the rotor blades to a different orientation to clear obstructions, be sure that any rotor brake is off and carefully turn the rotor by grabbing a main rotor blade tip and "walking" it. *Never turn a tail-rotor blade by hand*.

If the aircraft is to be left overnight, neutralize cockpit controls and apply friction locks. Apply rotor brake if present, and/or

Fig. 16-2. The exhaust system should come in for close scrutiny on each pre-flight inspection, since bulges, cracks, or leaks of any kind can be dangerous.

secure blades with factory-supplied sleeves, supports, or tie ropes. Do not tie blades down in such a way that they bear hard against the droop stops. (Note: In the Enstrom helicopters, it is desirable from the standpoint of long Lamiflex bearing life to store the helicopter with the collective control raised slightly, rather than in the full-down position. Neutralizing the collective tends to eliminate adverse preloads on the main rotor elastomeric thrust bearings.)

Battery Service

Battery service is more important than it may at first appear, since in some helicopters, such as the R-22, the main rotor and engine tachometers are electrical, and a loss of electrical function leaves the pilot without rotor rpm information. Batteries rarely "suddenly go" inflight, of course, and your alternator is designed to power all electrical circuits even with a low battery (although it should be remembered that for an alternator to function, its field coil must be given a small charge); nonetheless, wet-cell-type batteries do need frequent inspection.

Lead-acid batteries for aircraft (helicopter) use are similar to car batteries, except that they come in 12-volt as well as 24-volt versions, and all come with caps (rather than being of the no-maintenance, never-add-water variety). As a rule of thumb, you should inspect your battery at least once every six weeks in cold weather, and once every four weeks (or more often) in hot weather. Lead-acid batteries self-discharge (from inactivity) far more rapidly in warm weather than in cool. During the discharge process, sulfation occurs, leaving a thin chemical film on the cells' plates. This film insulates the plates and thus reduces battery performance—not only in terms of delivering electricity, but in accepting it as well. It's difficult to recharge a badly sulfated battery.

For checking your battery you'll need a small hydrometer with a numeric scale, from 1.000 to 1.300 (approximately). A gravity reading of 1.275 to 1.280 can be considered indicative of a full charge (at 80 degrees Fahrenheit). Batteries should be recharged whenever the specific gravity falls below 1.225 (which corresponds to a 50-percent charge state). Charging can be done with an automotive-type charger if the battery is 12-volt, but a special 24-volt charger will be needed if the battery is a 24-volt type. The starting charge should be around four amps (or less). A trickle charge of up to 48 hours at one amp is allowable (so long as the battery itself doesn't get hot to the touch), but trickle charging between flights should be kept to a minimum. On recharging a battery, all cells should check within 0.050 gravity units of each other. If any cell varies more than this amount from each of the others, the battery is near the end of its service life and replacement should be considered.

On reinstalling a battery (and you definitely *do* want to remove it for servicing; recharging a battery in the aircraft is not a good idea), inspect terminals for cleanliness and remove any corrosion buildup with emery paper. Install the positive lead first, and the negative (ground) lead *last* and coat the terminal connections with Vaseline to stave off further corrosion. Make sure the top of the battery is dry. Neutralize any spills with baking soda and water. Fill cells only to the bottom split-ring portion of the case; *do not overfill* cells.

Remember when working with wet-cell batteries that such batteries contain concentrated sulfuric acid and generate explosive gases (hydrogen and oxygen), along with creating a spark potential. This combination makes all wet-cell batteries highly dangerous. Accordingly, you should have plenty of fresh water on hand—not just for servicing the battery's cells, but for treating acid burns on skin. Ideally, sunglasses or other eye protection should be worn when working near batteries. No smoking should be permitted, nor should work be done in confined areas or near electric motors due to the explosion hazard. In short, use extreme caution when working with wet-cell batteries, and be prepared to seek medical attention promptly in case of acid spills.

Engine Oil

Change engine oil every 25 to 50 hours or every six months (if less than 25 or 50 hours are flown in a six-month period), and if a filter is present, change it at the same time as the oil. Operators of turbocharged helicopters should change oil more often than those with normally aspirated engines, due to the extra heat, contamination, and mechanical burdens placed on the oil. (Oil exiting a turbocharger looks like dirty whipped cream.) If all-climate operations are expected, use a multigrade aviation oil such as Phillips X/C or Aeroshell 15W-50 (if approved by the manufacturer). It is important not to substitute automotive or synthetic oils for aviation-grade oils, except as permitted by the engine or helicopter manufacture. Aviation oils are formulated to produce fewer engine deposits than car oils, and in an air-cooled engine, that can be extremely important for avoiding preignition. Turbine engines, of course, have their own unique oil requirements; if you fly a turbine-powered helicopter (JetRanger, 500D, etc.), adhere closely to the oil servicing recommendations given in your operating handbook or maintenance manual.

Regardless of the type of oil you use, it is sound practice to submit regular samples of (old) oil to a lab for spectrum analysis to determine contamination levels. Many labs around the country specialize in oil analysis. (Your shop can recommend one, or you can write to Cleveland Technical Center, 13600 Deises Ave., Cleveland, OH 44110 or Spectro, Inc., P.O. Box 16526, Ft. Worth, TX 76133.) For $10 to $15 a sample, you can have your old oil analyzed with regard to the concentration (in parts per million) of iron, aluminum, silicon, and other contaminants of interest and over a period of several hundred operating hours, you can determine trend lines for your engine so that any sudden deviation from normal will be evident immediately, tipping you off to possible engine trouble well in advance of inflight difficulties. Even a one-time oil analysis can be useful if the engine is concealing a broken ring or has ingested large amounts of dirt (silicon). A regular oil-analysis schedule should be a part of every helicopter operator's maintenance regimen.

Tail Rotor Gearbox Oil

In many helicopters, tail rotor gearbox oil is checked on the daily preflight inspection; and when it falls below a specified minimum level, fresh oil must be added. (Check your pilot's operating handbook or service manual.) In the Robinson R-22, if the sight gauge does not fill with oil when the tail of the helicopter is pulled all the way down, oil must be added as follows:

1. Remove safety wire from filler plug located on top of gearbox.
2. Obtain Robinson P/N A257-2 gearbox oil in the needed quantity.
3. Add oil through the filler opening until oil is visible in sight gauge, but do not overfill beyond this point. (*Note*: Most times, less than a teaspoon of makeup oil is needed.)
4. Reinstall filler plug, making certain gasket is in place.
5. Safety-wire plug as before. Be sure wire applies tension only in a plug-tightening direction.

Transmission Fluid

Most piston helicopters have an oil-lubricated transmission with self-contained oil supply. This oil supply must be checked regularly, and new oil added when the level falls below minimum. In the Hughes 300, the oil quantity is checked using a dipstick located on the right side of the transmission. The dipstick has two gradations: FULL and LOW. Also, a locking device is incorporated to preclude the dipstick's coming out of the transmission for any reason in flight. Makeup fluid is added through a filler port forward of the dipstick. The port has a spring-loaded cap. Total quantity of the system is three U. S. quarts.

The Hughes 300 operating handbook lists several approved transmission oils along with the ambient temperature ranges in which they are to be used. Since some of the approved oils are mineral-based, while others are synthetic, it is never permissible to mix fluids (which means the operator—namely, you—must know in advance what kind of transmission oil the helicopter has been serviced with). It's important to remember not to open the transmission access ports in dusty conditions, since transmission gears are highly vulnerable to erosion and fatigue caused by particulate (dirt) contamination. Maintain sanitary conditions at all times when servicing the transmission and if a relatively large amount of makeup fluid is needed (more than half a pint), inspect the transmission carefully for signs of leakage.

Lead-Lag Dampers

Main rotor lead-lag dampers are typically oil-filled (viscous) dampers with definite service intervals and inspection requirements. In addition to being checked on the preflight inspection, these dampers must usually be removed from the helicopter and purged of fluid periodically; in addition, the dampers must be disassembled and inspected at periodic intervals. (Consult your operating handbook or maintenance manual for details applicable to your helicopter.)

In the Hughes 269A and 300, individual blade dampers are used, each of which employs a combination of rotating and fixed friction plates held in compression and surrounded by oil. (The Enstrom's blade dampers are of the more conventional piston type.) The Hughes 269A/B dampers come with sight windows for judging fluid level. When the fluid level falls below the minimum (i.e., below one-half the window), makeup fluid should be added using a simple hand-pump-type oil can filled with MIL-H-5606 or MIL-H-6083 hydraulic fluid. It is necessary first to clip the safety wire on the filler plug and remove the plug along with a vent screw; then, after fluid has been added, the screw is reinstalled and the filler plug re-safetied. A visual check should be made for leakage before and after each servicing of the damper.

Windshield Care

In a helicopter, there is plenty of plexiglass to care for, naturally, and the plexiglass—in addition to representing a sizable investment of dollars, in terms of replacement value—is the pilots' only connection to the outside world if the helicopter is not equipped for instrument flight, hence *must* be kept in good condition if visual contact with the ground is to be maintained. This is extremely important for operators who fly in marginal weather or at night, naturally; and in pinnacle, rooftop, or confined-area operations, good visual contact with ground reference points is an absolute must.

Hence, glass must not be allowed to become fogged, scratched, crazed, or sooty or dirty.

The acrylic plastic of which helicopter windshields are made is very sensitive to mishandling and can easily be scratched. In addition, it can be crazed or even dissolved by exposure to a variety of solvents. Under no circumstances should a helicopter windshield be allowed to come in contact with: gasoline, benzene, carbon tetrachloride, ammonia-containing window cleaners, thinners, acetone, or MEK (methyl ethyl ketone). Oil or grease stains on plexiglass may safely be removed with a cloth moistened in kerosene. All other deposits should be washed away with soapy water, or plain water. Remove watches and rings from hands before working on windows; use the palms of your hands to wipe away dirt while washing the windshield with water. Use a damp chamois to dry the windows; do *not* use dry cloths, which will build static and attract new dirt.

Once the windshield is clean, it can be waxed with a nonabrasive-type hard-film paste wax (such as Turtle Wax). Between waxings, the plastic should be given a light rubdown before each flight with Mirror Glaze or Johnson's Pledge aerosol. Avoid paper towels, if at all possible; use flannel cloths instead. Turn cloths frequently to avoid dirt buildups that can scratch plexiglass.

Small scratches in plexiglass can be removed by diligent application of toothpaste and water (using a finger, not a toothbrush). When plexiglass has become extensively scratchy or fogged, it can often be restored to like-new condition through application of Micromesh (Micro-surface Finishing Products Inc., Box 456, Wilton, IA 52778). The Micro-mesh system employs varying coarsenesses of "cushioned abrasive" pads, each of which removes the scratch pattern induced by the previous grade, until in the end no scratches are visible in the plastic. The method is time-intensive, but it is the same method preferred by many airlines for restoring plexiglass to like-new condition—and in my experience, it works.

The same people who make Micro-mesh also market a superb anti-static cream and liquid polish. *Note*: When applying any wax or restorative, never use a rotary buffer or orbital vibrator; such a device is apt to leave fishhooks in the plastic. Instead, always use straight-line hand motions.

Grease Fittings

On the Hughes 300 there are at least 47 pilot-serviceable grease fittings (located at the rotor head, tail rotor, control system bottom end, and landing gear), the majority of which require service every 50 hours. Some of these lube points use MIL-G-25537 oscillating-bearing grease; others use heavy-duty general-purpose (MIL-G-23827) grease. Special-purpose greases are also called out for some applications.

Under FAR Part 43, pilots may legally apply grease points on an aircraft as preventive maintenance. Because of the large number of such lube points on a helicopter, rotorcraft operators stand to save a good deal of money doing this bit of maintenance themselves. There is a right way and a wrong way to apply grease, however.

Once you've learned the types of grease your helicopter needs for various locations in the drive system and control system, procure one grease gun for each type of grease and keep it filled with fresh lubricant of the proper variety. When it comes time to apply grease, clean the Zerk fitting (or grease nipple) thoroughly to prevent forcing dirt into the lube area. Then connect the grease gun to the fitting and inject grease into the bearing area until old grease starts oozing out of the bearing. *Continue applying grease until new grease appears to ooze from the bearing.* This purging of old grease is necessary to remove trapped wear particles that may have accumulated in the old grease. Merely applying small makeup quantities of grease to a bearing isn't good enough; rapid wear and loss of tolerances will be the end result.

After you've purged a bearing of old grease, you will of course be looking at an unsightly mess. Wipe up the excess grease when you're done, unless you want that grease to be flung at great velocity all over nearby structures when the helicopter is next flown. Many greases, such as MIL-G-23827, contain chemical preservatives that attack paint; hence it is important, not just for cosmetic reasons but for paint longevity to clean away any excess of grease after relubricating a bearing.

Elastomeric Bearings

Since the early 1960s, helicopters have benefitted substantially from the substitution of *elastomeric bearings* for conventional grease-packed roller and ball bearings in the rotor head area. Much of the early work in this field was underwritten by the U. S. Army, and for years, only larger helicopters used elastomeric bearings to any large degree, due to their cost. Now, however, even small helicopters can be found with elastomeric bearings. One light helicopter that uses them with great success is the Enstrom F-28.

Elastomeric bearings come in various designs (spherical, conical, cylindrical, etc.), but the basic construction in each case is characterized by the bonding together of alternate layers of elastomer (rubber) and metal laminate (which may be aluminum, titanium, steel, or brass). The alternate, paper-thin layers are formed and bonded in a variety of ways, the choice depending on the anticipated load factors and environmental conditions. Generally, elastomeric bearings are used to deal with oscillating loads rather than purely linear or rotational loads.

At first, the concept of using rubber or rubberlike compounds as a thin-film lubricant in a sandwich-like bearing may sound ludicrous, but rubber does possess the quality referred to by lubrication chemists as *high internal mobility*—which is a fancy way of saying that the molecules are fluid and free to move, giving rise to great elasticity. Under appropriate (high) loads, the rubber in the layers of laminate "gives" just the right amount, allowing smooth relative motion between parts, while also providing all the benefits of a sealed bearing.

What are some of the benefits of elastomeric bearings? First, elimination of brinnelling, galling, and pitting associated with conventional bearings. Secondly, reduction of vibration (due to the natural shock-absorbing characteristics of the elastomers). Third, no oil or grease is required—the bearing can never go dry (nor create a mess). Fourth, environmental resistance is good, because the unit acts as a sealed bearing. Fifth, a high degree of control over stiffness is attainable in the manufacture of such bearings, with proper choice of materials and thicknesses. A reduced parts count usually results from the use of elastomeric bearings as well. And most importantly of all, extended service life is the rule rather than the exception with elastomers: a TBO life of five times that of any conventional bearing is not uncommon (which tends to make up for the elastomer's high initial cost).

The Enstrom F-28 series uses elastomeric bearings made by TRW in the pitch-change area of the rotor head; they are referred to as *Lamiflex* bearings. (The use of these bearings is in part responsible for the Enstrom's extremely low maintenance requirements in the main-rotor area.) The Enstrom's Lamiflex bearings operate under fantastic centrifugal loads and absorb a high degree of mechanical-rotational forces and aerodynamic feedback involved in cyclic and collective pitch changes.

Because they contain rubber, elastomeric bearings usually have a five-year shelf life. Once installed on a helicopter (such as the Enstrom F-28A), however, such bearings are usually an IRAN item with no fixed retirement life. Routine service consists solely of a visual inspection for evidence of possible delamination. If visual inspection suggests deterioration of the bearing, or if there is evidence of Lamiflex bearing failure in flight (noted by the pilot as blade crossover or combined lateral-vertical "beat"), the diagnosis can be confirmed by temporarily uncoupling each blade's pitch-change linkage (at the upper end, by the walking beam arm, in an Enstrom) and attempting to hand-rotate each blade about the pitch axis. If the Lamiflex bearing is in good condition, the blade will offer moderate resistance and will tend to return to neutral pitch on being let go. If the Lamiflex bearing is bad, the blade may offer extreme resistance to twisting and the blade will tend to "stick" in one position when let go.

Lamiflex bearings of the same part number may be replaced individually on blades as needed in service. Lamiflex bearings of different P/N series may not be interchanged individually, however; instead, all blades must be converted to the new part number at the same time.

Certain preventive practices on the pilot's part can increase the life of Lamiflex bearings. First, high-airspeed cruise operation (i.e., near redline) should be avoided except for occasions when it is absolutely necessary. (In the Enstrom F-28 series, cruise airspeeds below 90 mph will give improved Lamiflex bearing life over operation at 100 to 107 mph.) Secondly, at the end of each flight the collective pitch control should not be locked in the full-down position, but instead should be repositioned to neutral (zero blade pitch angle). Otherwise, the Lamiflex bearings will be subjected to adverse preloads in storage.

Turbochargers

Many piston helicopters employ turbochargers to increase the power available for high-altitude and/or hot-day operations, and to increase the margin of performance in HOGE situations. The Enstrom F-28C, for example, uses a small Rajay turbocharger to recover exhaust energy from the Lycoming HIO-360-E engine and convert it to usable manifold pressure. In normal operation, the turbocharger rotor achieves speeds of up to 80,000 rpm and glows cherry red. Obviously, such an engine accessory carries with it certain maintenance needs.

First, there is a special need for adequate preflight inspection of the engine compartment, since in a turbocharged helicopter (much more so than in a normally aspirated helicopter) otherwise-acceptable oil leaks and seepage can create a serious fire hazard. Accordingly, the operator of a turbocharged helicopter should take special pains to see that oil and fuel leaks do not have a chance to start, and that all fluid-carrying hoses are properly clamped and protected from chafing, vibration, excess heat, etc. Also, the helicopter's exhaust system should come in for close scrutiny to detect bulges, cracks around welds, and greenish stains indicating exhaust leakage. Clamps should be inspected for good condition, and Rajay turbo housing should be examined periodically for hairline cracks. A leaking turbo housing has a blowtorch-like effect on nearby accessories and must be avoided at all costs.

If the system has a variable wastegate, the wastegate butterfly should periodically be lubricated with Mouse Milk, Amsoil spray, or other suitable penetrant oil. Also, every 10 hours or so (oftener, if possible) an attempt should be made to turn the turbocharger turbine wheel by hand to ascertain whether it is rotating freely. A dragging rotor may indicate bearing problems (turbo coking) or interference between the turbine wheel and scroll or housing.

If an exhaust gas temperature gauge is available in the cockpit, it should be calibrated and the engine operated at a mixture rich enough to keep the EGT below 1,650 degrees Fahrenheit at all times. Keeping exhaust temperatures low will have a definite, positive effect on turbocharger longivity.

Any time it is suspected that debris (in the form of sand, cotter pins, or what have you) has entered the engine, the turbocharger should be removed and a thorough bench inspection made, since the debris will almost certainly have come in contact with the rapidly spinning turbocharger rotor on the way out of the engine— and anything that hits a turbine wheel spinning at 80,000 rpm is likely to cause some damage.

A very important rule of thumb with regard to turbo operation is to *avoid hot shutdowns*. At the conclusion of every flight, idle the engine for a minimum of four minutes (or until cylinder head temperatures have gone well below cruise indications) to give the turbine a chance to spool down under full lubrication. The head soakback that occurs after a hot shutdown can easily bake the oil around the turbine shaft, causing what's known as "turbo coking." Hot shutdown is also bad for exhaust valves, in that it encourages valve sticking. Do your engine a favor and idle it for several minutes before each shutdown.

Finally, don't expect miracles from your turbocharger in terms of service life. Under mild duty-cycle conditions, a small turbocharger can be expected to go 1,200 hours or more without service; but in a typical helicopter application, a small turbo will need overhauling every 600 to 800 hours, or sooner in some cases. Budget accordingly.

Vibration Troubleshooting

Vibration is an inescapable fact of life in helicopters. There is no such thing as manufacturing a rotating part to zero tolerance levels, or balancing a part perfectly, or achieving perfect damping; consequently, there is no such thing as a vibrationless helicopter. There will always be some vibration due to the large number of moving parts. The best that can be done is to attempt to correct excessive vibrations as they become apparent. A certain amount of residual vibration will simply have to be tolerated.

How much vibration is too much? This requires experience. Whenever you're in doubt as to whether a new vibration is potentially serious, ask a veteran pilot or mechanic to fly the ship and comment on it. Once person's "alarming vibration" is another's minor annoyance.

Troubleshooting and correcting a helicopter vibration can be painstaking, time-consuming work, even for a professional helicopter mechanic with years of experience. It is not a job for an airplane mechanic—or a pilot, for that matter. A knowledgeable pilot can, however, save a professional's time by properly diagnosing unusual vibrations and describing them accurately.

Vibrations in helicopters are often classified in three groups: low-frequency, medium, and high-frequency. (These areas were touched on briefly in the chapter on Emergencies.) Low-frequency vibrations in the range of 5 to 10 Hz (one Hertz equals one cycle per second) are usually associated with imbalance of the main rotor, since the rotor itself spins at the rate of 300 to 500 rpm or five to eight revolutions per second. A vibration that occurs once per revolution of the main rotor is noticed by the pilot as a "one-per-rev" beat or pulsing. This pulsing can be purely vertical (felt mainly in the seat of the pants), or purely lateral (felt as stick shake), or a combination of both. A vertical vibration is usually associated with poor blade tracking. A lateral vibration, in contrast, is most often due to an unbalanced condition.

There are also, of course, two-per-rev, three-per-rev, and higher-order vibrations, the three-per-rev and higher orders usually being found in helicopters having three or more main rotor blades. Fourth-order and higher vibrations usually can't easily be counted by the pilot, however, since the vibration is at too high a rate.

Medium-frequency vibrations, falling approximately in the 50 to 2,000 Hz range, can be noticed as anything from a distinguishable beating or rapid pounding to a rattle or buzz. At 3,000 rpm, a piston engine is rotating 50 times per second and—if it has four cylinders—is producing two power pulses per crankshaft revolution; hence, a rattling vibration in the 100 Hz region is most likely to be associated with the helicopter's engine or transmission. Ignition problems (e.g., fouling spark plugs) and cooling fan distress are typical areas giving rise to medium-frequency vibration.

High-frequency vibrations are any vibrations occurring at a rate of 2,000 Hz or above. Sometimes these vibrations can only be felt as a tingling sensation. This sort of buzzing is often noted in stationary components (perhaps the anti-torque pedals) which may be vibrating in sympathy with the primary offender, most commonly the tail rotor or tail rotor gearbox. It takes a high degree of expertise and experience with a particular model of helicopter to diagnose and troubleshoot these kinds of vibrations quickly.

Rotor Imbalance

Rotor imbalance gives rise to a lateral (usually one-per-rev) shake, often accompanied by stick-wagging. It can be due to one blade flying high, problems with a lead-lag damper, or—in two-bladed, teetering rotor systems—improper chordwise or spanwise balance of the blade system as a whole. Obviously, anything that tends to put the rotor system's center of gravity off-center from the centerline of the hub will give rise to a lateral imbalance. For the most past, correction of rotor imbalance is beyond the province of the non-A&P-rated pilot. However, the competent helicopter pilot should be able to recognize the symptoms of lateral imbalance and be able to describe it accurately to a mechanic.

In helicopters with three or more rotor blades, lateral imbalance often occurs during the transition from idle to takeoff rpm, in a well-defined rpm range that is characteristic of the particular rotor system and helicopter involved. This is of course the ground resonance regime. If a helicopter's landing gear dampers (oleo struts) are working properly, the transition through this rpm range will be accompanied only by a momentary, low-amplitude oscillation of the airframe at around one to four Hz. If either the ship's lead-lag dampers or the landing gear struts are not working properly, however, the helicopter may tear apart in a matter of seconds as it enters the ground-resonance regime. Any undue vibration in this regime is immediate cause for grounding the ship until lead-lag dampers and oleo struts have been looked at and repaired.

When lateral shake is due to spanwise rotor imbalance, the technique most often used for achieving proper balance is taping the tips of the blades and feeling the change due to the added mass of the tape. (Note: It is impossible to correct an imbalance condition if the blades are not in track. Therefore, before attempting the following procedure, ensure that the blades are tracking correctly; see section below.) Usually, the helicopter manufacturer will specify the width and type of masking tape to be used, the location (blade station) it is to be applied, and the number of wraps that will be equivalent to the blade weights that will later need to be added. The usual procedure is to add two or three wraps of tape to one blade, run up the helicopter, and note whether the vibration got better or worse, then proceed from there. In the end, small washers or weights will be added to the "light" blade, and the tape removed.

In recent years, the troubleshooting rotor imbalance has been rendered easier by electronic balancing techniques (or accelerometer testing). The Chadwick-Helmuth Company of El Monte, California markets a system that has become very popular. It consists of a strobe light, a test meter box, magnetic pickups, and piezoelectric-type accelerometers which can be installed on a temporary basis in a relatively short time (either at the main rotor or the tail rotor; both rotors can be troubleshoot). During successive ground runups, the Chadwick-Helmuth tester gives azimuth and intensity (amplitude) information that can easily be plotted on special graphs to pinpoint the relative location of the vibration (in terms of being at 12 o'clock to the reference blade, or three o'clock, or eight o'clock, etc.) and amount of vibration in inches per second (IPS). In other words, the device tells you which blade is "light" and how much weight needs to be added to it. In as few as two ground runs, it is usually possible by this method to reduce a vibration to acceptable levels (less than 0.1 IPS).

While electronic balancing can also be attempted in the verticle axis (accelerometer mounted straight up and down) to detect the location of a poorly tracking blade, it should be emphasized that the Chadwick-Helmuth system is primarily a *balancing* system, not a tracking system. Since tracking must be accomplished first, before balancing attempts can be made, the electronic balancing method cannot be counted on as a total, all-in-one method or cure-all for getting a rotor to run true.

Rotor Tracking

Without a doubt one of the commonest—and hardest to troubleshoot—sources of vibration in helicopters is that due to faulty blade track. Like blade imbalance (above), faulty blade track usually doesn't "just happen" but occurs after some change to the helicopter (removal and reinstallation of parts after maintenance, for example, or replacement of a main rotor blade). Therefore the first step in dealing with suspected blade-tracking problems is to inspect the rotor system for damage, or any surface irregularity of the blades that could cause airflow disturbances. Blade-track problems are somewhat harder to troubleshoot than blade-imbalance problems, since the latter almost always gives rise to a purely lateral vibration, while the former can produce vertical vibration and/or lateral vibration—and can do so only in hover, or only in forward flight, or both (and at frequencies ranging from one-per-rev to three-pre-rev or more). What's more, every make and model of helicopter has its own unique blade tracking procedures and idiosyncrasies. Therefore, only very broad guidelines can be given here.

One rule of thumb that applies more or less equally to all helicopters is that when rotor imbalance or track problems are suspected, attempt to correct *track* first, then work on balance, unless the rotor is of a teetering two-bladed type and the entire rotor is off the machine (in which case it should be statically balanced and swept first, before installing it on the ship). The reason for this is that blade track vibrations can be so pronounced that they totally obscure lateral imbalance problems until the track problem is resolved.

In speaking of tracking, it is important to distinguish between ground tracking (tracking the blades while running the ship on the ground) and inflight tracking. Low- as well as high-rpm ground tracking may need to be done, and during the inflight phase, hover tracking and forward-flight tracking may be called for, since some vibrations occur only in one or the other regime. The manufacturer will usually specify an rpm for ground tracking.

Several methods are in use for ground tracking—e.g., flag and stick methods, reflector method, electronic strobe, and pre-track or "master blade" method. (The latter is done in a test cell and is most often employed at the factory in adjusting a blade's flight path relative to a "master blade" of known-good track.) The strobe and reflector methods—one involving a flickering light timed to the main rotor, and the other involving a continuous light gun shined on different-colored reflectors at the blade tips—are preferred, since they can be employed on the ground, or in the air.

As a rule, tracking involves changes both to the pitch links at the blade roots, and to the small trim tabs that are usually present at the trailing edges of the blades. Tabs should be bent only as described in the manufacturer's service manual, and only a uniform manner with no ripples in the metal. (Often a tab bender is supplied as a special service tool.)

Also as a rule, ground tracking involves changes to the blade pitch links (i.e., lengthening the links to decrease blade pitch; shortening them to increase pitch). Trim tab adjustments, by contrast, are confined to the inflight tracking phase. (In some instances, the manufacturer specifies two ground-tracking rpms—low and high—with pitch link adjustments coming during the low-rpm check and tab adjustments occurring in the high-rpm ground phase.) Pitch links often come with different thread coarsenesses at opposite ends, for fine and coarse adjustment of blade track. Unless otherwise noted by the manufacturer, trim tabs should be in neutral position before ground tracking is begun. *Consult your service manual before attempting any tracking operation, and abide by the advice contained therein.*

Once the proper ground track has been achieved by adjustments to the pitch links—a process that can involve numerous runups and shutdowns—vibrations at flight rpms can be trimmed out by appropriate adjustments to blade trim tabs. You will notice that many helicopters have more than one trim tab per blade. As a rule, the outermost tabs are intended for adjustments in high-rpm ground tracking and/or hover. The innermost tabs, in contrast, are adjusted to achieve proper high-speed inflight tracking. The Hughes 500C rotor blade, to give one popular example, has a single, long tab running the length of the blade at the outermost 65 inches of radius. This tab is divided by the manufacturer into six zones, each of which is treated differently for blade tracking purposes. The outermost 22 inches of each tab is never to be bent at all. The next two segments inboard can be bent in two-and-a-half-minute increments of arc as necessary to achieve proper high-rpm ground tracking; the one-foot-long segment of tab just inboard of the previous segment is adjusted for inflight tracking at cruise speeds below 100 knots; and the final two inboard segments are adjusted in high-cruise tracking (100 to 120 knots).

All of this is necessary because a rotor that ground-tracks well may not track at all in hover; and one that tracks in hover may not track well at high cruise speed. In forward flight, the dynamic variations on each blade are different than in a hover, and a "heavy" blade will behave differently in cruise than it would in HIGE mode. *Blade crossover* or *climbing blade* are the names given to the latter phenomenon. (Both mean the same thing; in flight, one blade flies through a greater range of vertical travel than the others, although all may track the same on the round and in a hover.) If that doesn't confuse you, there's also the paradoxical fact that the *low-flying* blade in a round-track check usually turns out to be the *high-flying* blade in a forward-flight check! Climbing-blade problems used to be more common in wooden-rotor days than they are now, but with metal rotor blades there is still enough variation in elasticity, blade twist, center of mass, torsional rigidity, and other parameters to give rise to climbing-blade syndrome now and then. A climbing blade doesn't necessarily constitute a hazard in and of itself, but due to Coriolis effects, the unusual vertical flight path of a climbing blade puts a heavy burden on lead-lag dampers and gives rise to some very annoying combined lateral and vertical shakiness.

Once again: Be sure to follow manufacturer's recommendations closely, and always *adjust track before trying to address rotor imbalance.*

17
Taking the FAA Flight Test

The requirements for obtaining a private pilot license with rotor-craft/helicopter privileges (or for adding the rotorcraft/helicopter rating to an existing private or commercial pilot's license) are spelled out clearly in Part 61 of the Federal Aviation Regulations. Among other things, the person wishing to qualify for private pilot helicopter privileges must be 17 years of age or older, must possess at least a third-class medical certificate, and must have logged a total of at least 40 hours of flight time, with at least 15 hours of solo time in helicopters. The flight time must include:

- [ ] A takeoff and landing at an airport that serves both airplanes and helicopter traffic.
- [ ] A flight with a landing at an off-airport site.
- [ ] Three hours of cross-country flying, with one flight covering three or more points, each separated by at least 25 nautical miles.

If commercial helicopter privileges are sought, the applicant must be 18 or over, hold a second-class medical certificate, and must have logged at least 150 total flight hours, including at least 50 hours in helicopters. The flight time must include:

- [ ] At least 100 hours as pilot in command (in helicopters or airplanes), with a cross-country flight involving three airports, each located a minimum of 50 nautical miles from the others.

☐ At least 40 hours of flight instruction, of which 15 hours must be in helicopters.

☐ A minimum of 10 hours as pilot in command of helicopters, including five takeoffs and landings at night, three off-airport landings, and landings at three airports that serve both airplane and helicopter traffic.

In addition to these basic requirements, an applicant for a private or commercial helicopter license (or rating) must pass a written test, an oral exam, and a flight check by an FAA inspector or designated examiner. Usually the oral exam and flight test are combined.

Naturally, the day of the flight test is a big day in the life of any helicopter pilot. All the hours of training, nights of studying for the written exam, and many postflight briefings held with instructors and fellow pilots come together on the day of the flight test; it finally all comes down to one flight. The flight test may last 30 or 40 minutes, or it may go on for over an hour. But in the end, either a white temporary license bearing the words "Rotorcraft: Helicopter" will be granted, or it won't. Getting that white slip of paper is what it's all about.

Unfortunately, a good deal of confusion surrounds the FAA flight test (or "practical exam," as it's sometimes called). The aim of this chapter is to demolish some myths concerning the FAA's flight test procedures and point out exactly the maneuvers and performance guidelines considered appropriate by FAA for the private and commercial helicopter check ride, based on FAA Advisory Circular 61-59A.

Preliminaries

You should know several things about how the FAA's check ride system works. The FAA itself has only a relatively small number of qualified helicopter examiners on its staff, and usually these individuals are also qualified in many other areas and have numerous additional responsibilities. It is physically impossible, in other words, for FAA to actually conduct every flight test for every helicopter license or rating granted in this country. Hence, the FAA designates highly qualified civilians, at the local level, to give flight tests in lieu of the FAA's own personnel. These proxies, officially known as FAA Designated Examiners, draw no salary from FAA and do not actually "work for" the government; they are private individuals engaged part-time (or, in a few cases, full-time) in the administration of FAA flight tests for profit. The fee charged by Designated Examiners can vary quite a bit, since the FAA has no direct control over what the individual chooses to charge. At the time of this writing, a typical fee for a private-pilot helicopter check ride is $90—and you supply the helicopter.

Another thing you should understand about the FAA flight test system is that the Designated Examiners are free, to a large degree, to test you on just the items the examiner feels he or she needs to test you on; the choice of test items is at the discretion of the examiner. In most cases, the examiner will interview the applicant's instructor (who will usually be present before and after the test—but not on the check ride itself) extensively, to ascertain that certain maneuvers have been adequately covered, and to get an idea of the applicant's overall competence in the helicopter. The pilot's logbooks, of course, will also be read carefully by the examiner before the flight to verify the applicant's compliance with Federal Aviation Regulation requirements.

It's important to try to see the check ride from the examiner's point of view. Most examiners are good-natured, easygoing people who like to fly and like to see others get a chance to fly; that's the business they're in, after all. No examiner *wants* to see an applicant fail a ride. The image of the gruff, sadistic drill-sergeant type is perhaps applicable to some military examiners, but civilian examiners are rarely, if ever, hostile or grim. The examiner is genuinely *on your side*—he wants to see you pass. (Examiners who fail a larger-than-normal percentage of applicants are given a close look by the FAA, and most examiners, being aware of this, try to avoid standing out.)

By the time the student has been signed off for the check ride (your instructor must actually sign what amounts to an affidavit affirming that you are ready to be licensed), he or she has been found competent in a wide variety of areas—much wider than could be tested in a single short flight—and the examiner, being well aware of this, is not interested in needling the applicant with tedious, time-consuming "hoop-jumping" exercises designed to explore every facet of the applicant's skill and training. It's too late for that. Instead, the examiner wants to see, mainly, whether you are a safe operator. He or she will be looking for common sense, sound judgment, and the ability to recognize an unsafe condition when it exists. The examiner will *not* be primarily testing you to see if you can fly a helicopter. If he had any doubt as to this, he wouldn't risk his life by getting in the ship with you! (Most will gladly tell you this.)

During the oral portion of the exam, therefore, be as relaxed as possible and converse naturally with the examiner, as you would converse with your instructor or with a fellow pilot. Don't be overly technical or self-critical in your responses to questioning. The examiner isn't trying to "grill" you, but instead just wants to see that you know and can recognize the importance of the most basic safety factors in helicopters operation—weight and balance considerations, density altitude's effects, the difference between HIGE and HOGE, etc. You aren't expected, nor will you be asked, to give detailed technical explanations of transverse flow or compressibility or other esoteric matters.

During your flights with your instructor, you were able to log the time only as dual; your instructor had to sign the logbook, since legally you could not fly as pilot in command with a passenger. On the check ride, however, you *will* be carrying a passenger (the examiner), and you *will be* the pilot in command. Don't expect the examiner to touch the controls; he's just there for a ride. He is *not* your instructor. As a matter of fact, if the examiner has to take the controls for any reason, there is a good chance you'll have failed the ride right then and there. *You are pilot in command during the entire check ride.* Act like it.

One more thing to remember: There's no such thing as *completely flunking* an FAA check ride (unless you forget to bring required paperwork or for some other reason are unable to even get started). Under present rules, any portion of the oral *or* practical tests that you pass the first time—even if you fail later sections of the exam—cannot be "taken away" from you; on a retest, you will only be tested in those areas where you did not do well before. FAA regulations require that you receive additional instruction in any areas that gave you problems on a flight test, but even so, it is often possible to get the instruction and be back to take the remainder of the flight test the *same day*. The main thing is that all is not lost if you should stumble on an item. Whatever parts of the test you pass, you pass forever.

Flight Test Checklist

Before appearing for the flight test, you will want to be sure the following items are on hand and ready available:

- ☐ Aircraft Airworthiness Certificate (required by law to be carried in the aircraft at all times).
- ☐ Aircraft registration certification (required on board the aircraft).
- ☐ FAA approved Helicopter Flight Manual (required on board the aircraft).
- ☐ Operating limitations, if any (required in the form of placards).
- ☐ Weight and balance data for the helicopter (required to be carried).
- ☐ Aircraft maintenance records (not required, but should be available for inspection).
- ☐ FCC radio station license (required by FCC rules if the aircraft has two-way communications capability).
- ☐ Pilot certificate.
- ☐ Medical certificate.
- ☐ Written test results.
- ☐ Logbook with instructor's endorsement.
- ☐ Signed application for flight test.
- ☐ Flight school graduation certificate (if applicable).
- ☐ Examiner's fee.
- ☐ Aeronautical charts.
- ☐ Computer and/or plotter.
- ☐ Flight plan forms and flight logs.
- ☐ Any tools needed to perform the preflight inspection (mirror, magnifying glass, screwdriver).
- ☐ Checklists.

Performance Evaluation Guidelines

Complete guidelines for the helicopter flight test are given by the FAA in *Private Pilot Practical Test Standards*, FAA-S-8081-1 (List ID: PPPTS-1A), $18.50 from the Superintendent of Documents, U. S. Gov't. Printing Office, Washington, DC 20402. For space reasons, we will not recount all the material contained in that publication; however, the following quotations bear on the subject of general flight test guidelines:

FAA states that "Emphasis will be placed on procedures, knowledge, and maneuvers which are most critical to a safe performance as a helicopter pilot. Unnecessary or avoidable flight into the caution/restricted areas of the 'height-velocity curves' as a result of careless operation shall be considered disqualifying. During all maneuvers, the applicant's ability to maintain proper rpm will be carefully evaluated . . . areas of particular importance include spatial disorientation, collision avoidance, and wake turbulence hazards." As stated further above, the examiner will be looking to see that you are able to identify potentially hazardous situations, and take the appropriate evasive actions, well in advance of actually encountering them.

Furthermore, FAA states: "The ability of an applicant for a private or commercial pilot certificate, or for an aircraft or instrument rating on that certificate, to perform the required pilot operations [of the test] is based on the following:

"1. Executing procedures and maneuvers within the aircraft's performance capabilities and limitations, including use of the aircraft's systems.
"2. Executing emergency procedures and maneuvers appropriate to the aircraft.
"3. Piloting the aircraft with smoothness and accuracy.
"4. Exercising judgment.
"5. Applying aeronautical knowledge.
"6. Showing the mastery of the aircraft, *with the successful outcome of a procedure or maneuver never seriously in doubt.*" (Emphasis added.)

Areas to be Tested

There are either eight or nine main areas in which helicopter applicants are tested (depending on whether the applicant is going for the private or commercial rating). These include preflight actions; airport and traffic pattern operations; air work (straight-and-level flight, climbs, turns, and descents); normal and crosswind takeoffs and landings; hovering, maneuvering by ground references, and air taxiing; running takeoffs and landings, and quick stops; recovery from settling with power (commercial applicants only); cross-country flight; and emergencies. We will discuss each of these areas in turn below. But as stated in FAA Advisory Circular 61-59A, p. 2. "There is no intention that the applicant be tested on every procedure or maneuver within each pilot operation, but only on those considered necessary by the examiner to determine competence in each pilot operation." What's more, "When, in the judgment of the examiner, certain demonstrations are impractical, competence may be determined by oral testing." In addition, "Throughout the flight test several procedures/maneuvers may be evaluated concurrently; i.e., traffic patterns, straight-and-level flight, climbs, descents, and turns." In other words, you will be expected to combine certain maneuvers and perform them competently at the same time, if the examiner tells you to do so.

With these caveats aside, let us take a look at some of the maneuvers you may be asked to perform in the course of your practical examination. We will paraphrase the FAA's own explanation of the relevant test areas, as given in AC 61-59A.

Preflight Actions

Objective: To determine that the applicant can ensure that the pilot requirements are met, that the helicopter is airworthy, and that suitable weather exists for the proposed flight.

Areas of interest: Certificates and aircraft documents, helicopter performance limitations, weight and balance, weather, line inspection, service requirements, and pretakeoff check of engine and systems. The applicant may be asked to produce the ship's papers and may be orally quizzed on operating procedures, flight limitations (if any), and fuel and oil servicing requirements of the helicopter in question. The applicant may be asked to determine the effects of wind, temperature, gross weight, etc. on helicopter performance based on charts in the Pilot's Operating Handbook. A hypothetical weight and balance problem may be posed. The applicant may be asked to obtain area and terminal forecast, sequence reports, NOTAMs, winds aloft, and/or other pertinent information from a Flight Service Station briefer. A visual inspection of the helicopter must be performed with the aid of a checklist. After engine startup, the applicant may be asked to demonstrate the checklist procedures for determining the airworthiness of the engine, control system, and other equipment.

Acceptable performance guidelines: The applicant shall use an orderly procedure in conducting a preflight check of the aircraft, recognizing any unsafe condition and explaining to the examiner the significance of each item checked. The applicant shall know the grade and type of oil, fuel, and hydraulic fluid specified for the helicopter, and will be required to know the amount of fuel required for the flight. The applicant should know the location, purpose, and significance of each item of the ship's required papers, and know how to work a weight-and-balance problem. In addition, the pilot must know what weather information is pertinent for the flight, where to obtain it, and how to interpret it. During the startup and runup, the applicant will be evaluated on the use of proper (checklist) procedures and his/her ability to ascertain the airworthiness of helicopter systems, controls, and equipment. Careless operation in close proximity to obstructions, personnel, or other aircraft shall be disqualifying.

Airport and Traffic Pattern Operations

Objective: To determine that the applicant can safely and efficiently conform to established arrival and departure procedures at controlled and uncontrolled airports, and can make takeoffs and landings competently under various field and wind conditions.

Areas for testing: The applicant may be asked to demonstrate the use of two-way communications equipment, including the use of Airport Terminal Information Service, ground control, tower, and/or Unicom frequencies, and ATC light-gun signals, as appropriate. Where available, the applicant may be asked to demonstrate the use of wind and traffic direction indicators, and markings indicating closed runways, taxiways, holding lines, etc. Safe procedures will be used in the vicinity of other aircraft, people, or property. The applicant may be asked to demonstrate arrival and departure procedures appropriate to the airport in use. Normal and crosswind takeoffs from a hover, and normal and crosswind approaches and landings on the airport, may be requested. The applicant may be asked to demonstrate a maximum performance takeoff from the surface, using maximum allowable power. On approach, the applicant may be asked to demonstrate a steep approach flown at an angle greater than that of a normal approach (approximately 15 degrees) and terminating in a stabilized hover at a designated spot. Collision avoidance practices will be exercised as appropriate. Likewise, the applicant may be asked to explain how, where, and when wingtip and rotor vortices are generated (for purposes of avoiding wake turbulence), and courses of action to avoid wake turbulence and minimize rotor downwash effects when operating near other aircraft on the airport surface.

Acceptable performance guidelines: The applicant shall determine the type of communications facilities available, select correct frequencies, and use appropriate communications procedures to obtain necessary information for operation in the airport traffic area. (Failure to comply with tower instructions will be disqualifying.) The applicant shall demonstrate a knowledge of standard wind and traffic direction indicators, runway markings and lighting, etc., and how they relate to helicopter operation. (Failure to properly use these aids, resulting in unsafe operation, will be disqualifying.) The applicant shall air-taxi the machine in compliance with local taxi rules and/or tower instructions, avoiding turbulence generated by large aircraft and exercising due caution in the vicinity of people or property. During traffic-pattern operations, the applicant shall apply proper corrections for drift, maintain adequate spacing, and adhere to prescribed altitudes (plus or minus 100 feet for private; 50 feet for commercial) and airspeeds (plus or minus 10 knots, private; 5 knots, commercial). The rotor or engine rpm will be held to plus or minus 50 rpm of that recommended (private and commercial). Drift during climbout shall be less that one rotor diameter, for private applicants (half a diameter, commercial) when within 10 feet of the ground, and plus or minus 50 feet (private) or 25 feet (commercial) when operating more than 10 feet above ground. Use of incorrect pedal to counter torque after climb will be disqualifying.

During the approach phase, the applicant shall establish and maintain the proper approach angle (approximately 12 degrees), airspeed, and ground track requested. Rpm will be held to within plus or minus 50 rpm of that recommended. Side drift when above 10 feet of altitude shall not exceed 50 feet for private applicants, or 25 feet for commercial pilots. Below 10 feet altitude, drift must be less than one rotor diameter (private) or half a rotor diameter (commercial). The use of incorrect pedal corrections to compensate for torque will be disqualifying.

During the maximum-performance-climb phase, performance shall be evaluated on the basis of accurate coordinated control application to achieve a smooth transition from a position on the ground to a steady-state climb. After reaching a height of approximately 50 feet above ground, a smooth transition should be made from max-rate to normal climb. Abrupt or uncoordinated control movements, or failure to achieve maximum performance, shall be disqualifying. Heading will be held to within 10 degrees for private applicants or 5 degrees for commercial applicants. In all cases, rpm shall be held to within plus or minus 50 rpm of that recommended. (*Note:* Penetration of the height-velocity curve is normal during execution of this maneuver. The maneuver may not be required if the flight test is accomplished in a helicopter that has the "height-velocity" graph contained in the operations limitations of the FAA Approved Flight Manual.)

During the steep approach phase, performance shall be evaluated on the applicant's ability to establish and maintain the desired approach angle, airspeed, and ground track, and avoidance of settling with power. Excessive drift or faulty coordination of controls shall be disqualifying. Heading should be held within 10 degrees for private applicants, or 5 degrees for commercial pilots. Rpm is to be held to within plus or minus 50 (all applicants). Circle termination shall be within 10 feet for private pilots, or 5 feet for commercial pilots. (*Note:* Penetration of the height-velocity curve is normal during this maneuver. The maneuver may not be required if the flight test is conducted in a helicopter which has the "height-velocity" graph contained as a part of the operating limitations in the FAA Approved Flight Manual.)

In the collision avoidance area, performance shall be evaluated on the basis of the applicant's vigilance in searching for other aircraft and reaction time in taking evasive action; also, the applicant will be expected to visually clear the area before initiating turns, and acknowledge receipt of ATC traffic advisories, when given. Failure to maintain proper traffic surveillance and separation shall be disqualifying.

With regard to wake turbulence, performance shall be evaluated on the applicant's ability to identify the conditions and locations in which wingtip or rotor vortices may be encountered and to adjust the helicopter's flight path so as to avoid these areas. Failure to follow appropriate procedures for avoiding flying into wake turbulence, or failure to minimize the effects of rotor downwash in the vicinity of small aircraft on the surface, shall be disqualifying.

Air Work

Objective: To determine that the applicant can competently maneuver the helicopter while monitoring instruments and outside references.

Maneuvers: The applicant may be asked to maintain selected headings, altitudes, and airspeeds. Also the applicant may be asked to demonstrate changes in altitude, heading, or airspeed. Power and attitude should be varied as necessary to control airspeed and altitude, not only in level flight, but in the entry and recovery from banked turns.

Acceptable performance guidelines: In straight-and-level flight, altitude shall be held to within plus or minus 100 feet for private applicants, or 50 feet for commercial pilot applicants. Airspeed shall likewise be held to within plus or minus 10 mph (private) or 5 mph (commercial); heading shall be held to within 10 degrees (private) or 5 degrees (commercial) of that assigned by the examiner. Rpm shall be held to within 50 rpm of that recommended, for all applicants. During climbs and descents, altitude at level-off should be within 100 feet of that assigned for private applicants, or within 50 feet for commercial applicants. Airspeed must be held within 10 mph for private applicants, 5 mph commercial; and heading must be maintained within 10 degrees for private pilots, 5 degrees for commercial pilots. Rpm must be maintained within 50 rpm of that recommended.

During turns, altitude shall not vary more than 100 feet for private applicants, or 50 feet for commercial applicants. Airspeed shall remain within plus or minus 10 mph (private) or 5 mph (commercial); angle of bank, within 10 degrees (private) or 5 degree (commercial); and heading on rollout, within 10 degrees (private) or 5 degrees (commercial). Rpm tolerances shall be plus or minus 50 rpm of that recommended.

Normal and Crosswind Takeoffs and Landings

Note: This is a required test item for commercial pilots, but optional for private pilot applicants since the private pilot will normally be examined for takeoff and landing ability in other phases of the flight.

Objective: To determine that the applicant can competently make takeoffs and landings in various wind conditions.

Maneuvers: The applicant may be asked to takeoff and landing various specified locations facing various directions.

Acceptable performance guidelines: Drift during climbout and on approach shall be less than half a rotor diameter when within 10 feet of the ground, and plus or minus 25 feet when operating more than 10 feet above ground. Use of incorrect pedal to counter to torque after climb or on approach will be disqualifying, as will failure to maintain rotor rpm within 50 rpm of that recommended.

Hovering, Air Taxiing, and Maneuvering by Ground Reference

Objective: To determine that the applicant can take off to a hover, perform hovering turns, and fly a precision pattern at hovering altitude, and air-taxi in compliance with local rules or tower instructions, as appropriate.

Maneuvers: The applicant may be required to demonstrate vertical takeoffs to a specified hovering altitude in headwind, crosswind, or tailwind conditions. Also, the applicant may be asked to perform vertical descents to a smooth landing, in headwind, tailwind, or crosswind conditions. In the hover, the applicant may be requested to demonstrate 90, 180, and/or 360 degree turns at constant altitude. The applicant may also be asked to perform precision patterns at hover altitudes (i.e., flight around a square, rectangle, or other ground reference). Demonstrations of forward, sideward, and rearward hovering flight may be requested. In taxiing, the applicant may be requested to air-taxi the machine along a designated route over the surface, or, at the examiner's discretion, he/she may be asked to move the helicopter in a sliding fashion on the surface from one point to another.

Acceptable performance guidelines: In the vertical takeoff phase, performance shall be evaluated on the applicant's ability to ascend straight up from the surface to a predesignated hover altitude with a minimum of forward, backward, or lateral movement over the surface. Heading shall be maintained to within 10 degrees of that assigned for private applicants, or within 5 degrees for commercial applicants. During liftoff, the helicopter's position over the starting point shall be maintained to within 10 feet (private) or 5 feet (commercial). Hovering altitude shall be maintained to within plus or minus two feet (private) or one foot (commercial). Rpm shall be maintained to within plus or minus 50 rpm for that recommended (all applicants).

In the vertical landing from a hover, the applicant shall be evaluated on his/her ability to descend to the surface smoothly, with a minimum of forward, backward, or lateral movement. The tolerances for heading, confinement over a point, and rpm shall be as set forth in the preceding paragraph.

During hovering turns, performance shall be evaluated on the applicant's ability to make both right and left hovering rotations while maintaining position, altitude, and headings within acceptable tolerances. Heading shall be maintained within 10 degrees for private applicants, or 5 degrees for commercial pilots. The helicopter's position over a fixed reference point should vary no more than 10 feet (private) or 5 feet (commercial). Rpm shall be held within 50 rpm of recommended (all applicants).

In the pattern-flying phase, performance shall be evaluated on the applicant's ability to fly the preselected pattern accurately while maintaining a safe altitude and keeping good control over heading and rpm. The desired ground track should be within plus or minus five feet for private applicants, or three feet for commercial applicants; headings should be kept within 10 degrees (private) or 5 degrees (commercial), as appropriate; hovering altitude should be maintained within plus or minus two feet (private) or one foot (commercial); and rpm should be held to plus or minus 50 rpm of the recommended rpm (all applicants).

While taxiing on the surface, performance shall be evaluated on the applicant's ability to maintain positive control of the helicopter, safely clear obstructions, and accurately move from one designated spot to another while the skids (or wheels) are in contact with the surface, maintaining a speed appropriate to existing conditions (but no more than five knots in any case).

While air-taxiing, the applicant's performance will be evaluated on the basis of maintaining positive control of the helicopter while moving at hover altitude. Obstructions shall safely be cleared and the assigned route accurately tracked. Ground speed shall be appropriate to the existing conditions (but no greater than 10 knots in any case). Rpm shall be held to plus or minus 50 of recommended.

Settling with Power

Note: This maneuver is required only for commercial applicants. However, settling with power may be covered in the emergencies section of the private-pilot check ride (see below).

Objective: To determine that the applicant understands and can recognize conditions of operation that result in a rapid power-on descent (settling with power) and can safely recover from such descents.

Maneuver: The applicant may be asked to explain the conditions of flight that result in settling with power, and explain the effects of various actions (including merely adding power) on recovery. The applicant may also be asked to demonstrate entry into this condition, with an *immediate* recovery initiation on the first indications of encountering the condition.

Acceptable performance guidelines: Performance shall be evaluated based on the applicant's demonstrated knowledge of and ability to recognize settling with power. Failure to immediately recognize the condition in flight shall be disqualifying. Also disqualifying will be any failure to apply prompt and appropriate recovery techniques to restore cruising airspeed.

Running Takeoffs, Roll-On Landings, and Quick Stops

Objective: To determine that the applicant has the control touch and coordination needed to safely take off and land under high-altitude conditions, and to safely perform quick stops.

Maneuvers: The applicant may be asked to demonstrate a take-off using less than hover power, thus simulating a high-altitude or high-gross-weight condition. The applicant may also be asked to make an approach and landing using less than hover power, for purposes of simulating "hot and high" conditions. In addition, the applicant may be asked to perform a rapid deceleration near the ground (with due consideration to height-velocity diagram information), terminating in a normal hover.

Acceptable performance guidelines: In the performance of running takeoffs, the applicant will be evaluated on his or her ability to properly coordinate the controls so as to achieve a gradually accelerating straight ground run to a point were translational lift is encountered, and thereafter, a smooth transition (using limited power) to normal flight, with normal climb speed being attained before exceeding an altitude of 10 feet. Throughout the maneuver, heading should be maintained to within 10 degrees in the case of private applicants, or 5 degrees for commercial applicants. Rpm shall be maintained within 50 rpm of recommended (all applicants).

During the roll-on landing phase, performance shall be evaluated based on the applicant's ability to establish and follow a shallow approach angle so that ground contact is made beyond and within 50 feet of a designated spot, in the case of private applicants, or 25 feet for commercial applicants. Performance shall also be evaluated on the applicant's ability to approach angle and to touch down smoothly in a level attitude while using less than hover power. Headings should be held to within plus or minus 5 degrees (all applicants). Rpm should be maintained to within plus or minus 50 rpm of that recommended.

During the performance of rapid decelerations (quick stops), the applicant will be evaluated mainly on coordinated use of the controls to achieve the desired helicopter performance. In addition, heading should not vary by more than 10 degrees in the case of private applicants, or 5 degrees for commercial pilots; altitude should not vary more than plus or minus 15 feet of that assigned for private applicants, or 10 feet for commercial applicants; arrival at predetermined termination point should occur within plus or minus 50 feet (private) or 25 feet (commercial); and rpm should be held within 50 rpm of that recommended (all applicants).

Cross-Country Flight

Objective: To determine that the applicant can adequately prepare for and conduct a safe cross-country flight.

Areas for testing: The applicant may be asked to plan a cross-country flight to a destination two hours away at the cruising speed of the helicopter to be used. At least one intermediate stop should be included. Planning should involve the procurement of pertinent weather and en route information; plotting a course on an aeronautical chart; selecting checkpoints; measuring distances; and computing flight times, headings, and fuel requirements. The Airman's Information Manual should be used as a reference for airport information. The applicant, once planning is complete, may be asked to make the proposed flight using dead reckoning, pilotage, and VOR and ADF radio aids as appropriate to the equipment installed in the helicopter. The applicant will be expected to make good the intended track, determine positive by reference to landmarks, and calculate estimate time of arrival over checkpoints. The applicant may also be asked to intercept and follow a VOR radial or an ADF bearing, recognize station passage, and determine position by means of triangulation with bearing fixes. (The applicant will not be asked to perform these procedures if competency has been demonstrated in previous FAA flight tests.) Finally, the applicant may be asked to divert to an alternate airport, as might be necessary for purposes of avoiding adverse weather. In diverting, the pilot may be asked to use pilotage, dead reckoning, or radio navigation, or a combination of the above.

Acceptable performance guidelines: Performance in the flight-planning stage shall be evaluated on the applicant's explanation of the plan for the flight, verification of calculations, and presentation of sources of information. In flying the flight plan, the applicant shall establish and maintain headings required to stay on course; correctly identify position; provide reasonable estimates of arrival times over checkpoints and destination (with an apparent error of not more than 10 minutes), and maintain cruising altitude within 100 feet of that specified for private applicants, or 50 feet for commercial applicants. In diverting to an alternate, the applicant shall be evaluated on the promptness of the action taken; and the applicant shall demonstrate an ability to compute, within a reasonable time, a new heading and estimate the flying time and fuel required to make the alternate.

Emergencies

Objectives: To determine that the applicant can recognize and react promptly and correctly to inflight emergencies.

Maneuvers: During cruise flight at traffic pattern altitude or higher, the examiner may close the throttle to simulate power failure. In response to this, the applicant should initiate an autorotation descent to an appropriate landing area. (A turn of up to 180 degrees may be made in the descent.) During a separate portion of the check ride, the examiner may choose to close the throttle during hover or forward air-taxiing, simulating a power failure; in response, the applicant should perform a hovering autorotation. The applicant may also be asked to explain or demonstrate the conditions of flight that can result in settling with power (see the section above on "Settling with Power"). Partial power failure may be simulated in flight by the examiner's limiting the engine power output to a level that will no longer support continued level flight; at which point the applicant should take prompt and appropriate corrective actions. Other areas of emergency operation that may be covered include:

1. Systems or equipment malfunctions. (The applicant may be asked to demonstrate his or her knowledge of corrective actions for such malfunctions as an inoperative electrical system, electrical fire or smoke in the cockpit, hydraulic failure, or inoperative trim, among other conditions.)
2. Navigational disorientation. (The applicant may be asked to explain the proper courses of action to be taken in the event of becoming lost, experiencing radio communications breakdown, or encountering unexpected adverse weather.)
3. Slope takeoffs. (Commercial applicants only may be asked to demonstrate a takeoff from a sloped surface.)
4. Slope landings. (Commercial applicants only may be asked to demonstrate a landing on a sloped surface.)
5. Confined area takeoffs. (Commercial applicants only may be asked to demonstrate a takeoff and climb from an area where the climb angle and flight path are dictated by wind, obstructions, and/or terrain features.)
6. Confined area approaches and landings. (Commercial applicants only may be asked to demonstrate an approach to and landing in an area where the flight path and approach angle are dictated by wind, obstructions, and/or terrain features.)
7. Pinnacle or rooftop takeoffs and climbs. (Commercial applicants only may be asked to demonstrate a takeoff and

climb from a small area that is higher than the surrounding terrain.)

8. Pinnacle or rooftop approaches and landings. (Commercial applicants only may be asked to demonstrate an approach to and landing on a small area that is higher than surrounding terrain.)

Acceptable performance guidelines: In the power-off autorotation, the applicant shall be judged on promptness of reaction and ability to safely complete an autorotation to a designated area where a safe landing could be accomplished. Arrival at the predetermined spot should occur within plus or minus 100 feet for private applicants, or 50 feet for commercial applicants; rpm should remain in the green arc (all applicants). Failure to lower collective pitch immediately after the power chop will be disqualifying. Failure to keep rotor rpm within the green arc will be disqualifying. An excessive rate of descent or faulty planning of the pattern shall also be disqualifying. (*Note*: Power recovery techniques will be used, since the FAA does not recommend full-on autorotations for practice purposes. Also, no simulated power failure will be initiated by the examiner in a place where an actual touchdown could not safely be accomplished should one become necessary, nor where an autorotative descent might constitute a violation of FARs.)

In the hovering autorotation phase, performance shall be judged on the applicant's ability to make a safe touchdown. Poor directional control, excessive drift, or subjecting the landing gear to severe side loads during the landing shall be disqualifying. Heading should be maintained within 10 degrees in the case of private applicants; 5 degrees for commercial pilots. A level attitude should exist at touchdown (all applicants).

Settling with power: See the "Settling with Power" section above.

In the partial power failure phase, the applicant's performance shall be evaluated on the timely initiation of an approach to the nearest suitable landing area using the power available, while making a methodical cockpit check to identify the cause of the power loss. If a landing ensues, the helicopter should touch down in a level deck attitude.

In a systems failure emergency, the applicant shall be evaluated on his or her ability to promptly analyze the situation and arrive at an appropriate course of action. Failure to apply normal corrective actions before declaring an emergency or initiating other drastic action shall be disqualifying, as shall any action which creates unnecessary additional hazards.

In a navigational-disorientation emergency, the applicant shall be judged on his or her ability to promptly assess the severity of the problem and take corrective steps appropriate to the situation.

In commercial maneuvers involving confined-area, slope, and pinnacle operations, performance shall be evaluated on the applicant's ability to demonstrate positive, accurate control technique with resultant good heading, drift, and altitude control. Headings shall be held within 5 degrees in all situations, and rpm within 50 of the recommended value. Poor directional control, mismanagement of rpm, sliding downslope, turning the tail rotor upslope, or attempting to land on a steep slope after mast-bumping occurs or full lateral cyclic has been applied shall be disqualifying, as shall poor judgment at any time. Failure to land at the selected rooftop or pinnacle touchdown point shall also be disqualifying.

Glossary

Glossary

advancing blade—As the rotor spins around its shaft, the blade turning into the wind is the advancing blade. If the helicopter is moving forward, the advancing blade will be in the right half of the rotor disc; if moving backward, it will be in the left; if moving sideward to the right, it will be in the rear half.

airfoil—Any surface designed to obtain a useful reaction from the air through which it moves in the form of lift. A streamline shape of aerodynamic surfaces which are designed to produce a minimum of drag and a maximum of lift.

angle of attack—The acute angle measured between the chord of an airfoil and the relative wind.

articulated rotor—A rotor system in which the blades are free to flap, drag and feather. A mode of attaching the rotor blade to the mast. A blade is said to be *fully articulated* when it's similar to the shoulder joint in its root attachment. This joint allows the rotor blade to flap up and down, move fore and aft to lead the lag and twist around its own axis in a feathering motion.

autorotation—Self-energized turning of the rotor. Unlike *windmilling*, where blade pitch is negative and energy is extracted from the rotor, autorotation is obtained with slightly positive pitch settings and no energy is extracted from the rotor. This creates maximum amount of lift.

bank—Sideward tilt of. It may be necessary to keep the craft from skidding, or side-slipping, during a turn. In a correctly executed turn, the bank compensates for the centrifugal force, and the pilot is pressed straight down into the seat, without any side force.

blade—One of the blades of the rotor. Usually more than just one is used. If the rotor has two or three or more blades, it's described as a two-bladed or three-bladed rotor, respectively.

blade damper—A device—spring, friction or hydraulic—installed on the vertical (drag) hinge to diminish or dampen blade oscillation (hunting) around this hinge.

blade loading—The load placed on the rotor blades of a helicopter, determined by dividing the gross weight of the copter by the combined area of all rotor blades.

camber—The curvature of the centerline of an airfoil. A symmetrical airfoil is said to have zero camber, because its mean contour is flat and the upper surface of the airfoil is a mirror image of the bottom surface.

ceiling—Maximum height to which a given helicopter can climb. Air is thinner at higher altitudes and the ceiling is reached when either the engine loses too much power or the blade airfoil begins to stall, or both. This happens at *absolute ceiling*. An altitude at which the craft still has the ability to climb 100 fpm is *service ceiling.*.

center of gravity (CG)—An imaginary point where the resultant of all weight forces in the body may be considered to be concentrated for any position of the body.

center of pressure—The imaginary point on the chordline of an airfoil where the resultant of all aerodynamic forces of the airfoil section may be considered to be concentrated.

centrifugal force— The force created by the tendency of a body to follow a straight-line path against the force which causes it to move in a curve, resulting in a force which tends to pull away from the axis of rotation. Applied to the helicopter, the force that would make the rotor blade fly out if it were not attached at the hub.

chord—The length of an airfoil as depicted by an imaginary straight line between the leading and trailing edges of that airfoil.

chordwise balance—An engineering term that refers to the mass balance of the airfoil. It's usually made to coincide with its center of lift. If this is not done, blade flutter could develop in flight, which might destroy the entire blade.

212

collective pitch control (collective)—Affecting all rotor blades in the same way. Collective pitch control changes the pitch of all rotor blades in unison, thus varying the total lift of the rotor. The method of control by which the pitch of all rotor blades is varied equally and simultaneously.

cone angle (coning angle)—The angle of rotor blade makes with the plane of rotation, similar to the dihedral angle of a fixed wing. Since the rotor blade is hinged at the hub, it's held out by centrifugal force, but since it also produces lift, it's deflected upward.

Coriolis effect—The tendency of a mass to increase or decrease its angular velocity, when its radius of rotation is shortened or lengthened, respectively.

cyclic pitch control—Repetitive once-around-the-circle change in the pitch angle of each rotor blade as it turns around the axis. Cyclic control is also known as "azimuth" control, and its purpose is to tilt the direction of lift force of the rotor, rather than to change its magnitude. The control which changes the pitch of the rotor blades individually during a cycle of revolution to control the tilt of the rotor disc and, therefore, the direction and velocity of horizontal flight.

damper—A mechanical device, similar to a shock absorber, installed on helicopters for the purpose of preventing the buildup of destructive oscillations. Dampers are found in rotorcraft in two critical areas: on the landing gear and on lag hinges of rotor blades. Without dampers, dangerous *ground resonance* would occur on many modern copters.

delta hinge (flapping hinge)—The hinge with its axis parallel to the rotor plane of rotation, which permits the rotor blades to flap to equalize lift between the rotor disc.

density altitude— Pressure altitude corrected for temperature and humidity. An altitude that's computed from the three H's (high altitude, high temperature and high humidity). Your craft performs like it's at the altitude, even though it's actually at a different altitude MSL.

disc—An area swept by the rotor blades. Although the rotor in flight actually sweeps a cone surface, for purposes of calculations, it's customary to speak of it as a disc. This is a circle, with its center at the hub axis and a radius of one blade length.

disc loading—Is similar to *wing loading* of a fixed-winger. It's the ratio of helicopter gross weight to rotor disc area (total chopper weight divided by the rotor disc area). The greater the disc loading the greater is the craft's sinking speed with power off and the steeper its angle of glide. Most helicopters are disc-loaded three to five, but some heavy cargo copters' disc loading goes up to 10.

dissymmetry of lift—The unequal lift across the rotor disc resulting form the difference in the velocity of air over the advancing blade half and retreating blade half of the rotor disc area.

fatigue—A property of structural materials, similar to that of human beings, which makes them break down under repeated stresses, while they wouldn't break down under stresses twice as high if applied only a few times. Vibration is the major cause of fatigue failures in helicopters. Because vibration cannot be completely eliminated from rotorcraft, fatigue is still the number one enemy of its designers and also the user.

feathering axis—The axis about which the pitch angle of a rotor blade is varied. Sometimes referred to as spanwise axis. Rotating around the long axis of the rotor blade, changing its pitch angle. In helicopters, feathering axis usually is designed to go through the quarter-chord of the airfoil to minimize control stick forces.

feathering action—That action which changes the pitch angle of the rotor blades periodically, by rotating them around their feathering (spanwise) axis.

flapping—The vertical movement of a blade about a delta (flapping) hinge. Rotor blades flap as much as eight degrees in forward flight. Without flapping, a craft would rollover on its side, because the advancing blade would produce more lift than the retreating blade.

flare (flareout)—A landing maneuver in which the angle of attack is increased near the ground; executed in helicopters as well as fixed wing craft and birds, which consumes the kinetic energy of forward velocity to arrest the descent. In a correctly executed flareout, horizontal velocity and vertical velocity come to zero at the same time, making a perfect zero-speed touchdown.

flutter—A self-induced oscillating motion of an aerodynamic surface, such as the main or tail rotors. It resembles, somewhat, the flapping motion of a bird's wings, Except that energy is extracted from the airstream rather than pumped into it. Noseweights on rotor blades are installed to prevent flutter. Occurrences of flutter in copters can be catastrophic and must be avoided at all costs.

freewheeling unit—A component part of the transmission or power train which automatically disconnects the main rotor from the engine when the engine stops or slows below the equivalent of rpm.

gimbal—A mechanism which permits the tilt of the rotor head in any direction, but restrains its rotation. If axes of tilt don't intersect the axis of rotation of a rotor, the gimbal is said to be *offset*. A correctly designed *offset gimbal head* allows the craft to fly hands-off for an unlimited length of time.

ground effect—The "cushion" of denser air confined beneath the rotor system of a hovering helicopter, which gives additional lift and, thus, decreases the power required to hover. It's the extra buoyancy near the ground, which makes the craft float a few feet off the ground on a pillow of air. Ground proximity does, in fact, increase the lift of a rotor up to the height of one diameter above the surface.

ground resonance—A violent "dance jig" that a helicopter sometimes develops when its rotor is turning while it stands on the ground. It happens only to choppers equipped with lag hinges and inadequate dampers. Lag motions of the blades become amplified by the flexibility of the landing gear, and the craft can destroy itself in a few seconds, if power is not shut off at once.

gyroscopic precession—A characteristic of all rotating bodies. When a force is applied to the periphery of a rotating body parallel to its axis of rotation, the rotating body will tilt in the direction of the applied force 90 degrees later in the plane of rotation.

hovering in ground effect (HIGE)—Maintaining a fixed position over a spot on the ground or water which compresses a cushion of high-density air between the main rotor and the ground or water surface and, thus, increases the lift produced by the main rotor. Normally, the main rotor must be within one-half rotor diameter to the ground or water surface in order to produce an efficient ground effect.

hovering out of ground effect (HOGE)—Maintaining a fixed position over a spot on the ground or water at some altitude above the ground at which no additional lift is obtained from ground effect.

hunting—The tendency of a blade, due to coriolis effect, to seek a position ahead of, or behind, that which would be determined by centrifugal force alone.

IRAN—Inspect and Replace As Necessary.

lag-lead—Motions of blades in the plane of the rotor around lag hinges. They were introduced on rotors with three or more blades to minimize severe, in-plane stresses caused by the difference in drag on the blade as it went from advancing to retreating positions. Not all rotors have lag hinges, some two-bladed rotors don't have them. They obtain the same lag-lead stress relief by using a flexible mast.

life—Maximum safe duration of operation of any part of a helicopter. It is limited by the probability of either fatigue failure or excessive wear. Life of ball bearings could be 10,000 hours; V-belts 500, rotor blades 2,000 hours, etc. Everything on a helicopter must be regarded as having limited life of uncertain duration, unless designed by qualified, professional engineers for unlimited life.

milking—A procedure for regaining main rotor rpm.

mast—Main structural member of the rotorcraft which connects the airframe to the rotor. In spite of its simple function, the mast must be very carefully designed to minimize the feedback of damaging vibrations between the rotor and the airframe.

noseweight—A lead weight attached to the leading edge of an airfoil. Its function is to prevent flutter.

pattern—In-plane lineup of rotor blades so they perfectly balance each other. For example, in a two-bladed rotor, if the line connecting the center of gravity of each blade doesn't pass through the center of rotation, the blades are said to be *out of pattern*. Such a rotor would develop a one-per-rev vibration similar to out-of-balance.

pitch angle—The angle between the chord line of a rotor blade and the reference plane of the main rotor hub or the rotor plane of rotation.

radius of action—Maximum distance a helicopter can fly from its home base and return, without refueling.

range—Maximum distance a helicopter can fly without landing or refueling.

redundancy—A fail-safe design which provides a second standby structural member should the main one fail, or providing two members to do the same function. Dual ignition in aircraft engines is a typical redundancy. Because doubling up of everything would be expensive in both the weight and money, engineers use redundancy only in those areas where the probability of failure of a single member is high, or where it would result in catastrophic damage.

retreating—Retreating blade is on the opposite side of the advancing blade. It travels with the wind created by the forward motion. If forward velocity of the craft is zero, and there is on wind, simply opposite the advancing blade.

retreating blade stall—A stall condition that can begin to affect inboard as well as outboard portions of the retreating blade during high-speed forward flight. The stall occurs as a result of excessive angle of attack due to aggravated blade flapping; corrective action consists of applying rearward cyclic.

reverse flow region—A small region at the inboard end of the retreating blade in which the relative wind is coming from behind the airfoil.

rigid rotor—A rotor system with blades fixed to the hub in such a way that they can feather but cannot flap or drag.

roll—Tilt of the rotorcraft around its longitudinal axis. Controlled by lateral movements of the cyclic.

rotor—The lift-producing, rotary-wing part of the rotorcraft. It consists of one or more blades and is correctly described as a two-bladed rotor, three-bladed rotor, etc. *Rotor blade* refers to a single blade only.

semirigid rotor—A rotor system in which the blades are fixed to the hub but are free to flap and to feather.

slip—The controlled flight of a helicopter in a direction not in line with its fore and aft axis.

solidity ratio—Portion of the rotor disc which is filled by rotor blades; a ratio of total blade area to the disc area. The ratio of total rotor blade area to total rotor disc area.

spar—The main, load-carrying, structural member of the rotor blade. It carries the centrifugal force as well as lift loads from the blade tip to the root attachment. A second spar sometimes is added for redundancy.

stall—Destruction of lift due to turbulent separation of airflow from the top surface of an airfoil, caused by excessive angle of attack. Stall can occur at any airspeed, given sufficiently high angle of attack.

standard atmosphere—Atmospheric conditions in which the air is a dry, perfect gas; the temperature at sea level is 59 degrees F (15 degrees C); the pressure at sea level (or reduced to seal level) is 29.92 inches Hg; and the temperature gradient is about 3.5 degrees F per 1000-feet change in altitude.

swashplate—A tilting plate, mounted concentrically with the rotor shaft. It consists of rotating and non-rotating halves, the rotating part being connected to the pitch horns of each rotor blade, and the non-rotating part to the cyclic. Thus the pilot can control the pitch of each blade while the rotor is turning.

teetering—Hinge and motion around it, in see-saw fashion, in two-bladed rotors. It allows one blade to flap up and forces the other blade to flap down. Use of teetering hinge allows direct transfer of centrifugal forces from one blade to the other, without going through the mast and separate flapping hinges.

tip path—The plane in which rotor blade tips travel when rotating.

tip speed—Airspeed at the tip of the rotor blade. Too high a tip speed is wasteful in power, too low a tip speed gives problems of controlling the retreating blade. Tip speed of small rotorcraft varies from 300 fps (200 mph) to 750 fps (500 mph). Lower tip speed yields greater lifting efficiency.

tip stall—The stall condition on the retreating blade which occurs at high forward speeds.

torque—A force, or combination of forces, that tends to produce a countering rotating motion. In a single rotor helicopter, where the rotor turns counterclockwise, the fuselage tends to rotate clockwise looking down on the helicopter). Anything that rotates and consumes power, produces a reaction torque in the direction opposite to its rotation. Tail (antitorque) rotors are added to helicopters to overcome torque produced by main rotor rotation.

tracking—Tracking of the rotor is an operation necessary to assure that every blade rotates in the same orbit. This means that each blade tip must follow the path of the preceding one. If not, a vibration will develop, which is similar to the dynamic unbalance of a wheel. To put a rotor *in track*, the trim tab of the low blade should be bent up and vice-versa.

transition—A narrow region of flight speed in helicopters, usually between 10-20 mph, when they slide off the ground cushion, and before they pick up the added lift of forward translation. The airflow pattern through the rotor changes erratically during transition and is often accompanied by roughness and partial loss of lift.

translational lift—The additional lift obtained through airspeed because of increased efficiency of the rotor system, whether when transitioning from a hover into horizontal flight or when hovering in a high wind.

trim tab—A small metal plate projecting behind the trailing edge, near the tip, of a rotor blade. Its purpose is to aid in tracking the rotor. Without trim tabs, the pitch of the entire rotor blade would have to be changed to adjust its track.

weave—A form of rotor-blade instability, which may be caused by excessive, elastic softness of the rotor blade or of the control system. When weave occurs in improperly designed craft, the rotor suddenly stops following the pilot's commands and darts, seemingly, out of control. Like flutter, it must not be permitted to occur in flight.

yaw—Turning of the helicopter right or left around its vertical axis. In helicopters, its done by changing the pitch of the tail rotor.

Index

Edited by Steven H. Mesner

Other Bestsellers From TAB

Other Bestsellers From TAB